Share You

How to write a life-changing book

…in 60 days!

by

Cassandra Farren

Welford Publishing

Published in 2018 by Welford Publishing

Copyright © Cassandra Farren 2018

ISBN: Paperback 978-0-9931296-6-7

ISBN: ebook 978-0-9931296-7-4

Author photograph © Kate Sharp Photography 2018

A catalogue for this book is available from the British Library.

Dedication

For Mum

I hope I have made you proud, x

Acknowledgements

To Kieron and Lennie, thank you for inspiring me to be the best I can be, so that I can be the best mum to you. I'm sure we will be celebrating with more cakes and raspberries soon!

To Sandie, who knew that the words you said to me back in 2012 would lead to setting up my business and writing three books?! Thank you for helping to change the course of my life and giving me hope, at a time when I was felt completely lost.

To Beccy, when we 'randomly' met online we were unaware of how our lives would so closely intertwine. Your friendship and generosity really does mean the world to me. Thank you for always being there for me, and for believing in my vision for Share Your World.

To Zoe, thank you for being the beautiful earth angel that you are, for supporting me through the tears and for being a true friend.

To Jacqueline, thank you for trusting that your author journey would be safe in my hands. I am so proud of not only what you have achieved, but the woman that you have become in the process.

Thank you to Michelle Emerson from Painless Online Publishing for editing and typesetting my book. Thank you for also being such a huge support to the authors I work with. You have such a warm and supportive way of making the self-publishing process effortless!

Thank you to Kim and Sinclair Macleod from Indie Authors World for designing my beautiful book cover.

About the Author

Cassandra, who lives in Northamptonshire, England, has been described as "a gentle soul powered by rocket fuel!"

When she's not mentoring authors or writing life-changing books, Cassandra can often be found relaxing by a beautiful lake or having a dance party in her kitchen!

She is a very proud Reiki master who has committed to her own journey of personal and spiritual growth.

Cassandra's mission is to create a new generation of heart-led authors who collectively make a powerful difference in the world, one book at a time.

Contents

Chapter 1

Life is not a fairy-tale

Once upon a time there was a girl named Cassandra.

Cassandra was not one of those girls who grew up in the land of 'Fake Believe!' She did not expect Prince Charming to sweep her off her feet and carry her into the sunset to live abundant lives filled with Pilates, Prosecco and Prada! But neither did she assume she would spend most of her adult life lurching from one failure to another whilst banging her head against a metaphorical brick wall. She questioned time and time again what she had done to deserve this chaos. What was her purpose? And had she been drunk before she agreed to come to earth and fulfil this purpose?!

From the outside looking in you would never have guessed that Cassandra often felt like an alien on planet earth. She didn't like to admit to herself, let alone anyone else, that she felt different. Despite the crazy rollercoaster journey that life had taken her on she always put on a brave face, remained positive and did her best to 'fit in'. But she didn't feel fulfilled.

Cassandra knew deep down that there was more to her and more to life, but how would she find this missing jigsaw piece? She realised that hiding from herself only led to feeling even more lonely, it was time to take responsibility and move forward with her life.

One sunny day in October 2012, Cassandra decided enough was enough. She was emotionally exhausted from trying to figure out everything on her own and booked a 'crisis coaching call' with a very intuitive lady called Sandie. Cassandra poured out her life story, hoping that Sandie would be able to help her make sense of the chaos and give her some guidance towards piecing her life back together. At the end of their lengthy phone call, Cassandra was shocked and stunned into a long silence. (Anyone who knows Cassandra will tell you this is a rare occurrence!)

There were three reasons for this unusual silence:

1) Sandie had explained to Cassandra that she was so much more inspiring than she realised, and it was little wonder her career hadn't worked out because she had been hiding herself away. It was now time to do this on her own.

2) Sandie also told Cassandra to write down her personal journey so far and that everything would make sense and fall into place.

3) Cassandra was convinced that Sandie had confused her with another coaching client. Surely, Sandie wasn't suggesting that she should start her own business when her last job was as a cleaner, she had ended her marriage six months previously, was now a single parent to two children, and had no financial resources? And how on earth was writing about these negative experiences going to help her move forward with her life?!

Thankfully, Cassandra had been brought up to be polite and respectful so instead of saying, "That is the craziest idea I have ever heard of, what a load of nonsense, I want my money back!" What she actually said was, "Ok, if you think it will help I will begin to write down my journey and I'll let you know how I get on."

That night Cassandra took a deep breath, opened a new Word document and began to write.

Three months after her 'crisis coaching call' with Sandie, Cassandra set up her own business, with nothing more than a Facebook page, hope and lots of determination.

And two years after those first words flowed from her heart and onto the page, Cassandra very proudly published her first book, *The Girl Who Refused to Quit.*

Being the down-to-earth and grounded girl that she is, Cassandra didn't expect to lead a fancy life when she became an author or assume she could sit back and happily retire off the royalties. Nor did she anticipate that her life would suddenly and very unexpectedly collapse for the third time, just a year after publishing her debut book.

She felt ashamed and embarrassed, and at one point contemplated writing a sequel called *The Girl Who Quit!* She doubted whether she had the strength to continue with her business whilst her life was in such a mess.

If anyone had told Cassandra that she would courageously rebuild her life and publish her second book, *Rule Your World,* she would have come out from her duvet, paused her 'Bridget Jones's Diary' DVD and laughed in their face!

And if anyone had told Cassandra that her books would receive over 100, 5* reviews on Amazon and that a few months after publishing *Rule Your World* she would be mentoring authors and writing her third book, *Share Your World,* she would have laughed even harder!

If you are reading these words right now in a real-life book or an e-book, then (Oh. My. Goodness!) she has actually gone and done it, woohoo!

***

Let's be honest, we both know that life is not a fairy-tale, in fact it can be damn hard at times but I (Cassandra) am living proof that you can release your past, give your life meaning and create your very own happy ever after.

I have had a battle with many demons in my mind over the years. When Sandie first suggested that I should set up my business my first question to her was, "Do I need to get a degree?" I honestly didn't think that anyone would take me seriously as a business owner without one.

When I decided I would write my first book the demons came out to play again. I questioned who was going to take me seriously as an author when I do not have any qualifications in writing (other than a GCSE in English) yet here I am confidently writing my third book on how to write a book!

My self-esteem and confidence have been at rock bottom many times. I felt like a failure as a mother after becoming a single parent for the third time in 2016. I felt like a failure as an employee, as no matter how hard I tried I could not find a career that worked for me.

Time and time again I have been knocked down in my life. How have I found the strength to carry on? I believe that you always have a choice in life, you can give up or you can get up.

I want to share my life philosophy with you, 'Do not allow the ghosts from your past to steal the happiness from your future.'

Your ghosts are not just people. They are the beliefs, emotions and fears that are holding you prisoner in your own life. They no longer serve you.

I believe that it is your responsibility to let go of your ghosts. It's time to stop allowing them to haunt your mind.

I believe that when you find the courage to let go of your old story and accept that your past does not define you, that's when you will give your life meaning.

Can writing a book give your life meaning?

I was reading an interesting article written by Emily Esfahani Smith, author of *The Power of Meaning*, who suggests that what makes our time on earth worthwhile is not chasing happiness but giving life meaning.

If you think about it have you ever maintained the feeling of true happiness for long periods of time? The reason that this is not sustainable is because happiness is an emotion that comes and goes, it can't be permanent.

This is Emily's definition of meaning;

"Meaning is always about connection, and about contributing to something greater than yourself. It's about loving other people and placing yourself at their service. The more you can forget yourself in the process, the greater your power to connect and to contribute, the more meaningful your life will be."

When I read Emily's definition I had a huge epiphany.

What is the meaning of life?

The meaning of life is to give your life meaning.

How can you do this?

Simple. Share Your World.

When you share the story of your life, you will quickly see how every single event and experience has led you to be where you are today.

You will see everything in a new perspective.

You will understand how your past, present and future all connect together.

Making peace with your past is a priceless gift you give to yourself.

Yes, you need courage. Yes, you need confidence. Yes, you need commitment.

But, you have not come this far on your journey to only come this far!

If you had to summarise your life in one sentence it would go something like this, "Well that didn't go to plan!" There have been many twists and turns along your journey. At times you were consumed by the dark thoughts that haunted your mind as you questioned if you would find your way back into the light. There have been people and situations that have pushed you to your limits. You have come close to breaking, but you are not broken.

One of the best things about your past is that it's in the past! It is just a story. I don't say 'just' to belittle what you have been through, but when you can see your past as a story it will begin to diminish its hold over you.

I truly believe that if you are reading this book then you are here for a reason. You know that you have a powerful message within you. I believe that it is my purpose to empower you to step up and Share Your World to help others who are still in the dark.

I will be (metaphorically) holding your hand as we go on this journey together.

By reading my book:

*You will discover why so many writers unnecessarily stay stuck in fear.

*You will learn a powerful way to beat procrastination, so that nothing will stop you from finishing your book.

*You will find out my powerful, proven author preparation steps which will connect you to your goal on a deep emotional level. If the going gets tough these will quickly enable you to get back on track.

*You will learn how to effortlessly release yourself from your past along with any trapped emotions, which will ensure the tone of your book remains upbeat and uplifting.

*You will discover how to create the perfect emotional space to write which will allow your words to easily flow out with ease. Goodbye writer's block!

*You will find out how to set the perfect physical space to ensure you always have a calm and enjoyable writing experience.

*You will have the courage and confidence to find your voice which will set your book apart from other authors.

*You will discover the secret of writing in such a compelling way that your readers will feel that your book was written especially for them.

*You will learn my simple technique to discover the purpose of your book and how to easily plan the outline for your chapters.

*You will find out how to remain consistently focused and motivated, so that at the end of 60 days you will have completed the first draft of your manuscript.

*You will know the next steps to publish your book once the first draft of your manuscript is written.

*You will discover my top tips to start marketing your book so that you can easily begin to Share Your World.

All of this will be broken down into manageable bite-sized chunks as I like to keep things simple.

Déjà vu?

If you have read my second book, *Rule Your World,* you will notice that some of the practical tools and techniques are also included in *Share Your World.*

If there was a small voice in your head that just whispered, "Is Cassandra being cheeky and sharing these tools again to increase her word count?" you can rest assured that this is not the case. You will find out in Chapter 5 why I choose not to follow the traditional publishing rules on word counts. I make no apologies for reminding you of these powerful tools that, when used on a regular basis, not only will make you a better writer, but also have the potential to change your life.

If I was the kind of girl to place a bet (which I'm not!) I would bet that even if you have learnt about my tools you haven't been using them every day. This will serve as a gentle reminder to not just know about these tools but also to implement them into your life.

My books are part of a series, so it is only natural that they will share some content and follow a similar format with my simple, pragmatic approach to writing.

Let's get this out in the open, I have a unique, holistic, approach to writing. I am proud of this and do not aspire to follow the crowd. Some parts of my writing process are not logical, and I make no apologies for that either. I have learnt from my own experience what works and what doesn't work when writing a life-changing book. Whilst this is not a full on "happy clappy, praise the Universe" kind of book, I will be combining my spiritual experience as a Reiki master and bespoke meditation-maker with my practical experience of writing and publishing three books. If you're open to a sprinkle of spirituality and want to learn my unique approach of how to write a life-changing book from the inside out, then you are in the right place.

You may like to think of me as your supportive Fairy Godmother, but before you get too excited about my special powers I must tell you this. If you follow my advice and implement the practical tools they will assist you in becoming a respected and renowned author, but I do not have a magic wand. It is your responsibility to take the necessary action required to ensure that your dream of making a difference in the world turns into reality.

Contrary to popular belief, writing a book does not have to be hard work. Am I saying that it is easy? Definitely not. What I am saying is that when you combine your burning desire to share your message with my proven techniques then nothing will stop you from releasing your past and becoming who you were born to be.

Are you ready to give your life meaning and create your own happy ever after?

Let's do this!

Cassandra x

P.S I'd love you to come and join my Facebook group www.facebook.com/groups/heartledauthors

Author Tip I will be sharing lots of practical information, so you may want to purchase a new notebook to keep everything together. You may as well treat yourself to a new beautiful pen as you will need this to sign your first book.

Chapter 2

Excuses, excuses!

If you had a pound for every time someone said, "You should write a book" you would probably be reading my book from a beautiful island in the sun, sipping exotic cocktails without a care in the world! You may have started to write down your ideas, you may have a plan, but something has stopped you from taking this any further.

I'd like you to answer the next two questions honestly;

1) How long have you been thinking about writing your book?

2) What is stopping you from writing your book?

I am guessing the answer to the first question is months or years as opposed to weeks or days and that the answer to the second question is a combination of the excuses listed below.

You may prefer to refer to them as 'reasons why you haven't started to write your book'. I am going to call them excuses! If you are honest with yourself, you know deep down that something has stopped you from getting started. Writing a book is a big deal and it is completely normal to feel apprehensive. The reason I can speak so confidently about this topic is because I have made many of them myself!

Let's get them out in the open.

Excuse #1: I haven't got the time to write a book.

Have you been telling yourself that there aren't enough hours in the day to write your book? I heard this fact on a webinar and it opened my eyes to how we all manage our time; We all have 24 hours in the day. If you sleep for 8 hours and you work for 8 hours, you still have 8 hours left! I understand that life comes with other responsibilities but when you step back and take a good long look at where you are choosing to spend your time you will be in a better position to know where you will find the time to write.

Be honest, how much time do you spend each day on social media? How much time do you spend watching television? Are either of these activities going to change lives? It may be that you choose to get up an hour earlier in the morning, it may be that you decide to write in the evening instead of watching TV or endlessly scrolling through your social media news feeds.

I'm going to share a secret with you, nobody has the time to write a book. If you are serious about becoming an author, you will need to find the time to write your book.

When you make your book a priority in your life you will make the time to write it.

Excuse #2: Who am I to become an author?

Many aspiring authors procrastinate due to The Imposter Syndrome;

"A concept describing individuals who are marked by an inability to internalize their accomplishments and a persistent fear of being exposed as a fraud."
- Definition from Wikipedia.

Can you relate to the feelings of 'Who am I to be writing a book?' 'Who is going to listen to me?' or 'Who is going to take me seriously?'

I suffered from The Imposter Syndrome with both of my previous books. I sat and cried the night before *The Girl Who Refused to Quit* went live on Amazon as I got myself into a panic thinking, 'who on earth is going to want to read this? It's just my life, I'm not even sure it's that interesting!'

I remember apprehensively arriving at my own book launch expecting to be 'found out' that I wasn't a real author!

You would have thought that by the time I began to write *Rule Your World* that I had got rid of those negative voices in my head but oh no, they were having a party and once again causing me to seriously doubt myself and my message.

You have only got to read the amazing reviews from both of my books to see that I was wrong to worry and that I was right to find the courage to keep writing and tell that negative voice to sit down and shut up! My books have helped so many people and you need to trust that yours will do the same. I believe the only way to overcome this fear is to stop over thinking everything and to start writing!

Excuse #3: Am I qualified to write a book?

Writing a book is a big deal but there is no one on this planet who is more qualified to write your story than you. You are the expert in your life and that makes you the expert to write about your life.

My last job was as a cleaner, prior to this I was a mortgage adviser, so becoming an author was not exactly a natural career progression. It is completely normal to question if you have got what it takes, only you hold the true answer to that, but hand on heart I believe that if I can do it, then so can you.

Excuse #4: I feel apprehensive about emotions that may come to the surface.

Sharing your personal journey is not for the fainthearted. You are putting yourself in a very vulnerable position. Many people can find it hard to talk about their life challenges, let alone find the courage to share these in a book for the world and his wife to read!

I'm not going to pretend that there won't be any tears along the way because that would be unrealistic. What I will share with you is that I know that writing my first book was a fundamental part of healing and releasing my past. There is something very powerful and cathartic about sharing your story in your voice. I believe that the more emotion you evoke as you write, the more powerful your book will become. Your ideal reader will not only read your words, she will feel the energy and emotion behind them. I believe it is imperative to combine your writing with ongoing healing and meditation as these will assist with releasing any trapped emotions that no longer serve you.

Free Author Meditation

I have made you a free procrastination buster author meditation to listen to as part of this book. I will be sharing more information about why meditation is so important in Chapter 3 but for now please go to **www.cassandrafarren.com/free-meditations** and download the *Share Your World* meditation.

You will find the courage to acknowledge and release any emotions that come to the surface. Always remember that by being brave and sharing your journey, your ideal reader will not feel so alone in hers.

Excuse #5: I feel overwhelmed by how to publish my book.

There is such a wealth of information on this topic that this section could become a book in itself!

I am going to provide a summary of the most popular ways to publish your book, but I would highly recommend that you spend time researching the options further to find the best one for you.

This is going to be the most logical part of the book. Hold on tight!

1) Traditional publishing

When authors are published through a traditional publishing house they receive instant credibility and a strong reputation. This is because you are published under a national or global brand which has trust and recognition, implying that your book is worth reading.

You work with a team of experts who will ensure your book is produced to a very high standard and will help you to market your book before launching it through their established contacts. There is a good chance of it being stocked in all the well-known book shops.

Traditional publishing houses publish a select number of books each year. They absorb the risk and they absorb the cost. They tend to pay an advance to the author, which is a payment based on projected future sales. The author then receives a percentage of each book sale once their book has generated enough sales to recoup the amount of their advance.

Hypothetical Example: Cassandra receives an advance of £5000.00, she will then receive £1 for every book sale (this is typically 10% of the list price per book) she would need to sell 5000 copies of her book before she begins to receive her additional royalty payment of £1 for every future book sold. Cassie would also sign over the rights to her book to the publisher for the length of her contract.

If you aspire to become traditionally published I recommend that you ask yourself the following questions:

Are you a celebrity? This could be a pop star, an Olympian or perhaps someone who has climbed Mount Everest in record-breaking time. Many celebrities will be offered a book deal because they are already in the public eye and have a trusted following of loyal fans who will want to buy their book.

Do you have a large online platform? If you have 15,000 (or more) followers on social media, your e-mail list or YouTube there is a good chance that a traditional publisher will be interested in speaking to you. (You will also need a great concept for a book!)

Do you want to have full control of your book? You will be working with a team of publishing experts, so you will tend to have less control over the content and overall look of your book.

Do you want to publish your book quickly? Publishing houses are extremely busy as they are working with multiple authors at the same time. They will have set procedures and timescales for each part of turning your manuscript into a book. If you were offered a book deal today it is unlikely that your book would be published until at least one year later.

Are you happy to market your book? It is likely that you will have some support from a PR and marketing team, but a traditional publishing house will still expect you to promote your book to your audience. This could be through social media, webinars, live events or speaking engagements.

Do you have high levels of confidence in yourself and in your book? The actual process of landing a traditional publishing deal can be very time-consuming, not to mention emotionally draining. Many publishers won't accept unsolicited manuscripts which means that you will need an agent to approach them on your behalf. You contact potential agents with a query letter and a short overview of your book. If they respond they will ask you for an in-depth book proposal, possibly a marketing plan and sample chapters from your manuscript. You then patiently wait for a response.

Once you have secured an agent they still need to find and secure you a publisher. This can be a very long and drawn out process which could erode confidence in yourself and in your work.

A very high proportion of manuscripts are rejected. Apparently, J K Rowling's manuscript was rejected 12 times before Bloomsbury offered her a book deal!

A real-life story

I used to dream of being offered a traditional publishing deal. Two years ago, I found out about a rare event in Manchester where I had the opportunity to pitch my book to a panel of commissioning editors.

I set off on an adventure, which consisted of six trains, two trams and a taxi, full of hope and excitement wondering if this could be my chance to get my book out to more people in the world. I was elated to be one of only four people chosen to go through to the next round. I then waited patiently to hear from them to let me know if they wanted to take it any further.

As the time passed I became more and more fixated on wanting the result of being traditionally published. When they eventually got back in touch to say they enjoyed my book, but they wouldn't be taking it any further I cried, and I mean really cried. I was so disappointed and lost a lot of confidence in myself and in my work.

Once I dried my eyes, pulled myself back together and told myself to get a grip I realised that this setback was not going to stop me from sharing my book with the world. I have self-published all of my books. I have concentrated on gaining amazing reviews and using my books as business tools to increase my work as a mentor for authors and as a professional speaker.

Would I consider a traditional publishing deal? Absolutely. If you are a commissioning editor who loves my books and would like to have a chat, feel free to e-mail me on hello@cassiefarren.com haha!

2) Self-publishing

If you aspire to self-publish your book I recommend you ask yourself these questions:

Are you prepared to invest in a team of publishing experts? When self-publishing first became popular there was an assumption that your book wasn't up to the standard of a traditionally published book. I believe that this was due to many authors jumping on the bandwagon, taking shortcuts and not investing the time, money and energy that their book deserved.

If you choose to self-publish please, please, please (does that sound desperate?!) invest in an editor, a proof-reader, someone to typeset your work and a professional book cover designer. It is a complete myth that people do not judge a book by its cover, they do! They also judge the quality of your writing, so it should not be full of grammatical mistakes.

You are investing so much of your time and energy into writing your book so please invest in the quality of your book. Your book is an extension of who you are so be proud of yourself, be proud of your work and produce it to the highest standard you can.

Are you ready to be your own project manager? When you choose to self-publish you will need to register your book with the British Library and get an ISBN number. This is the 13-digit number which identifies your book, usually found on the back of the book. You will also need to set up your book for print-on-demand distribution so that you, and possibly other wholesale companies, can order your book.

You will need to manage each step of this process until you are ready to press the button to order the first copy of your book. This does take a lot of focus and dedication, but what it also means is that you have full control over the timescale of when your book is published.

Are you ready to be your own marketing manager? Once you have found the courage to write your book and the strength to publish, you then begin the task of marketing it. There are many ways in which this can be done, and each book will have a different marketing strategy. The great news about marketing a self-published book is that you can be as creative as you like, you do not need to obtain permission from anyone else.

Do you want to use your book as a business tool? One of the benefits of self-publishing is the speed by which you can publish your book. I began writing *Rule Your World* on the 1st June 2017 and published it on the 1st November 2017. Did I acquire some new grey hairs during this process? Yes! Was it worth the slightly increased stress levels and new grey hairs? Absolutely!

If you are intending to use your book as a business tool, then the quicker you become an author the better. This can up-level your business immediately as you instantly become an authority (have you ever noticed that the word authority is 'author' with 'i t y' added?) If you want to speak at events you will have an advantage over other speakers who aren't authors. You may like to run your own events and have book signings.

Do you want to have control over the cost and flexibility of your book? You have the advantage that you can buy your books at cost price from your print-on-demand company.

You can make more money per book when you self-publish. The print cost of your book will vary depending on the size and format of your book but as an example I pay £2.25 per book for *Rule Your World* and sell a paperback for £7.99. (If you sell through a third party, such as Amazon, they will take a percentage of your profit.) If you use your book as a business tool this gives you the potential to add an extra income stream into your business by selling your books at events or from your website/social media.

It is unlikely that your book will generate vast amounts of most money for your business. Your book will give you expert status and credibility, whilst building trust and rapport with your ideal clients. This can lead to increased fees for speaking, coaching and mentoring and will set you apart from your competitors.

When you self-publish you can extend or re-print your book at any time. With my first book *The Girl Who Refused to Quit* I decided to add two additional chapters one year after it was first published. This was a simple process of writing and editing the chapters, typesetting the chapters and then uploading the new file to my print-on-demand company. As your business evolves you may want to have the flexibility to make changes.

You will also have the benefit of having creative control over your book. If you want to include your brand colours or you have a specific cover design in mind you have the final say on your book cover and the interior of your book.

A real-life story

I had a beautiful vision for the front cover of *The Girl Who Refused to Quit.* I had seen many influential women on social media in strong power poses, you know the ones where they have their arms stretched out in the air like they have just conquered the world! I decided that I wanted to be stood in front of a stunning sunset poised in a power pose. I enlisted the help of a local photographer, we set off to literally chase the sun as it began to set over a reservoir. It was one of the most beautiful sunsets I have ever seen, it was like everything had come together and it was meant to be, but we had to act fast as the sun was fading quickly.

I stood at the edge of the reservoir with my back to the camera as I held my best power poses. I remember feeling so proud of myself and was excitedly looking forward to choosing which photo would make it to the front cover. When the photos came through a week later the sunset was as stunning as I remembered, but instead of looking like a powerful warrior I looked like a human version of the Statue of Liberty! (NB this was due to my lack of power posing skills!)

Thankfully I remembered the photographer had taken some relaxed photographs of me before and after the shoot and I asked if she could send those over. As soon as I saw the natural photograph of me calmly looking out over the reservoir without a care in the world, I knew that would become my front cover. I have had so many compliments on my cover and I am so grateful that I had the final say on which image was used.

When you self-publish you retain all the rights to your book and have full control over your work from start to finish.

3) Co-operative Publishing

There are also companies that allow you to co-operatively publish your book. This could be viewed as a mix of the benefits of traditional and self-publishing. You write your book and then pay a fee to have your book published. There will be a team of their experts who will ensure that your book is produced to a high standard whilst producing your book in a much shorter time than if you were traditionally published. Most co-operative publishers will use a print-on-demand service, however you may be required to place a minimum order of books each time you order.

I highly recommend that you do some of your own research and decide which publishing route feels right for you, but in the meantime please do not let this stop you from writing. It is highly unlikely that you will ever get a book published without making a start on your manuscript!

Excuse #6: I've got so many ideas for so many books!

"Hi, my name's Cassandra and I'm addicted to having ideas for books!" Can you relate to this? I say this in a light-hearted way as my head is always buzzing with which book to write next (I already have the titles for my fourth and fifth books!).

It's great to be excited about writing and it's amazing to have lots of ideas flowing but please do not let that stop you from getting started, and more importantly, getting your first book finished.

You may have lots of pretty journals full of lots of great ideas. You may debate with yourself on a regular basis, should you start with your life-story or your self-help book? The chances are that neither are making much progress in transforming into a real-life book. You may find that you're feeling stuck and your words aren't flowing.

I believe that you should start by writing your life story. Your ideal reader wants to know that she can relate to you and the journey that you have been on before you start telling her how to change her life. I have read some self-help books that have one paragraph about the author, for me this isn't enough. I want to know who the author is and what they have experienced in life so that I know they understand me. I do not want to be spoken down to or fed endless generic information that I could have searched for online. I heard a quote that said, 'There are no unique messages, just unique messengers.'

You become a unique messenger when you share your story.

I feel that the world is crying out for real stories from real people. Your ideal reader wants to feel connected and understood. Yes, your life story is the book that requires the most courage, but it will give your ideal reader deep insights into her own life which have the power to begin the internal transformation she is seeking.

Excuse #7: Am I too young or too old to write a book?

There is no lower or upper age limit to writing a life-changing book.

I recently spoke in a local college where I met a very inspiring young man called Caleb Vuluvic. Caleb is sixteen years old and is currently halfway through writing his debut book, *Hush Hush*, which shares his inner thoughts of being a mute from aged three to fifteen. I have no doubt that by courageously sharing his personal story Caleb's book will make a big difference to many people's lives.

Louise Hay was 60 when she wrote her first book and she continued to write until she was 89!

If you have a strong desire within you to share your story, then now is the time. Your age is irrelevant.

Excuse #8: I don't have all of the answers.

Have you stalled in writing your book as you don't feel you have all of the answers, or that you haven't reached your final 'happy ever after?' When you share your experience, your feelings emerge in your voice, and that in itself powerfully assists your readers to find their own answers and encourages them to look inside themselves to gain new positive insights and lessons from your journey. In some ways I feel sharing your life story can be even more powerful than writing a self-help book. The reason for this is that if we are honest we don't always like being told what to do, even if we know we need to make a change. By sharing your world, you aren't telling anyone what to do but written in the right way your reader will find their own answers and feel empowered to make positive changes in their life.

A real-life story

This is one of my Amazon reviews from *The Girl Who Refused to Quit*:

"I totally blame this author for keeping me up past midnight because once I started this book I had to finish it in one sitting. Cassie has come through so much in her life. Haven't we all, though? But the difference is, she isn't quitting. From studying exams, to relocating, to taking jobs that weren't right for her at the time due to her commitment to her family, shows Cassie's strong work ethic and overcoming adversity. The refreshing thing about this book is that it is not a happy ever after ending. As we all know, life is a work in progress. And Cassie illustrates beautifully how things can change in an instant, and it's how you deal with these changes that matter."

This review emphasises the point that my reader liked that my life was still a work in progress.

Excuse #9: Why would anyone want to read my story? I am just me.

I get it. Before I published *The Girl Who Refused to Quit* I also questioned why anyone would want to read about the seemingly boring life of Cassandra from Kettering when they could choose to read about the seemingly elaborate lives of a multitude of well-known celebrities. Celebrity books will always sell, but will they change lives? A celebrity may have been through a similar experience but that little voice in your head may whisper, "well it's ok for her." Yes, she may have split up with her husband, is heartbroken and will now be a single parent but the chances are she's not being faced with being re-housed in an area she doesn't feel safe in due to no one wanting to privately rent to a single parent who is in receipt of housing benefit. I nearly spat my tea out when I read an interview about a celebrity who had recently become a single parent. She was understandably upset but then went on to share that "holidays were no longer the same". She had recently been abroad with a nanny, but she found it was a challenging time!

A holiday abroad with her children and a nanny was a challenging time, seriously!? My point here is not to have a rant. I'm not doubting that her life has changed, just like any other single parent, but my question to you is this, if you were to unexpectedly become a single parent feeling afraid and alone and uncertain about your future whose story would you rather read, hers or mine?

My belief is that everyone in the world is energetically connected. If you have been through a difficult time, I do not believe that you are the only person in the world to experience this challenge. It was after I published *The Girl Who Refused to Quit* that I had this insight. I realised that everyone who felt inspired to read my book had done so for a reason. They may not have all experienced exactly the same challenges, but they could all relate to my feelings and my journey in some way.

There is a real need for real people to share relatable stories. The most important part is being relatable. Whenever you go through a challenge in life you will find true comfort and gain insights from someone who you can relate to who has been through a similar experience.

Excuse #10: "My teacher/careers advisor/tutor etc told me…"

Fill in the blank;

"_____ told me I wasn't good at English."

"_____ told me I would never make anything of myself."

"_____ told me I would never become an author."

"_____ told me I was stupid."

These are some of the most popular excuses I hear. I want you to know that in this section I am writing assertively, with love, because I want you to know that you have a choice and that you do not have to be defined by your past. Right, that's enough of me trying to justify why I've put on my big girl assertive pants today!

For this section I'm going to refer to your teacher/careers advisor/tutor etc as 'the dream stealer'.

I have a question for you;

How old were you when the dream stealer told you that you weren't good at English, that you would never make anything of yourself, that you would never become an author or that you were stupid?

I'm guessing this was at some point in your childhood?

I have another question for you;

Do you still believe in the tooth fairy? How about the Easter bunny? No? Is that because you choose not to believe in made-up stories from your childhood? So why are you choosing to believe the made-up bullshit your dream stealer told you?

Yes, I swore and yes, I meant it! It frustrates me that so many people are allowing made-up stories from their childhood to steal the dreams from their future. Chances are you haven't seen or spoken to your dream stealer for many years. Chances are they haven't given a second thought to the nonsense that left their mouth many years ago. I'm not saying it's acceptable for people in positions of authority to make these throwaway comments.

Are you going to allow a made-up comment from your past to stop you from writing a life-changing book that will change your future?

I have another question for you;

How many compliments have you received since your dream stealer made their comment to you? You're not sure? If I was the kind of woman to make a bet (which I'm still not!) I would bet that you have received hundreds of genuine compliments but that 99% of them have been forgotten, deflected or ignored. Yet, you choose to remember, repeat and live by that one negative comment which was not even true!

Did your dream stealer tell you that you weren't very good at English?

Just because, in their opinion, somebody else thinks that you are not very good at English it does not mean that you cannot become a successful and respected author.

You need to share your experience and feelings with an underlying positive message of encouragement with your reader. You do not need to have an A* or a degree in English.

A real-life story

One month ago, I had to Google what a pronoun was to help my nine-year-old son, Lennie, with his homework! (I'm typing this now wondering if I can remember what one is and I can't haha!) So yes, it's official I admit that I, Cassandra Farren, do not know what a pronoun is! Yet here I am, confidently writing my third book with book number four and five in the pipeline!

It gets worse! Two weeks ago, I attended Lennie's parents evening and was sat outside his classroom reading through his English book. I enjoyed a piece of work he had written before reading this comment from his teacher;

"You included all of our important facts. Your sentences need some more work to include fronted adverbials."

What on earth is a fronted adverbial? I honestly have no idea. Lennie thought this was hilarious and did try to explain but again, this information has not been retained by my busy brain which potentially makes my nine-year-old son better at English than me!

Does this mean that I should shut down my laptop and quit writing the rest of my book? Of course not. I choose to believe that my message deserves to be heard, in my voice, and that my unique writing style will appeal to my ideal readers.

I will be sharing some more information on how to confidently write in your voice in Chapter 6 but until then I have said it before and I will say it again;

"Do not allow the ghosts from your past to steal the happiness from your future."

– Cassandra Farren (feel free to quote me on this!)

Harsh but true

You may want to ask yourself if you were using your dream stealer as a convenient excuse not to write your book, when deep down it's your own fears that are holding you back.

The same can be said for each and every one of your excuses, they are all hiding an underlying fear.

As I mentioned at the start of this chapter the reason I can be honest with you is because I have made so many of these excuses myself. It is natural to have doubts and fears but once you have finished reading my book I know you will have found the courage to finish what you've started.

This doesn't mean that you will never feel scared. It does mean that you will not let your fear stop you from achieving your goal.

How do you find a way of turning your 'excuses for not writing your book' into 'reasons why nothing will stop you from your book?'

If you want to find a way you have to find your 'why'.

I believe that writing your book does not need to be hard work, but it does require a lot of willpower. Unfortunately, you can't buy willpower; if anyone invented that they would be a billionaire! But don't give up hope. I will be sharing many tools throughout this book to help you develop several new positive habits. Until then I want you think about your 'why'.

Finding your 'why' creates an emotional attachment to your goal of writing a life-changing book. This is a fundamental part of your success as an author.

Practical exercise

To find your 'why' answer question 1 and keep on asking yourself "why?" until you reach an answer that has a meaningful connection to you; you may want to write your answers down.

My real-life example

Question: Why do you want to Share Your World?

Answer: I want to share my story in my words.

Why?

Answer: I want to prevent other women from feeling alone and afraid when they are experiencing unexpected challenges in their life.

Why?

Answer: I self-destructed and hated myself for many years and I hated the person I was. I want to empower other women to know that they can take back their control.

Why?

Answer: I want them to know that they hold the power to release themselves from their past and that they also hold the power to recreate their future.

Why?

If sharing my journey can make a difference to one person's life, then it will make everything I have been through worthwhile.

There is it! That's my 'why'.

It is very powerful and may initially seem unrelated to the initial question, but this is where the power lies which will fuel your willpower.

It's your turn.

Go through the questions above and find out why it is so important for you to write your book now. Go with your gut instinct and keep on asking yourself why, until you get to a reason that is meaningful to you. There may be times on your author journey when you feel like you are taking one step forward and two steps back, and that's ok, the way to get back on track quickly is to go back and remember your why.

Harsh but true

Excuses = the lies you tell yourself so that you feel better about justifying your lack of responsibility for not taking action in your own life.

Once you have obliterated your excuses and found your 'why' this is a huge step towards writing a life-changing book.

How can you take this newly acquired courage, determination and focus to the next level to ensure that your dream of becoming a respected author becomes reality?

Find out in Chapter 3!

Chapter 3

Put your pen down!

I repeat, put your pen down!

Have you ever wondered why so many people are apparently 'writing a book' but they never actually become an author? I believe that the main reason is because they can't keep their determination, focus and motivation long enough to see the end result.

Before you write (or type) the first word of your first chapter there are several important author preparation steps to take. I understand that you may just want to dive straight in and get writing but once you have followed my proven process and sit down to write, your words will flow out with ease.

I have already mentioned that my process is simple, but do not confuse simple with easy. You may wish to bookmark this page for any challenging moments when you may want to rip up your manuscript and put it in the bin!

We are going to build a solid emotional foundation for your book, so that if the going gets tough you can get back on track as soon as possible. I've had several sob 'n' snot moments with my last two books and I have a new box of tissues ready, just in case, whilst I'm writing this one!

It's perfectly normal to start out with lots of fresh motivation but as you know life has a funny way of trying to throw you off course when you set any long-term goals. It is imperative that when the 'I don't know if I can do this' moment strikes that you can quickly pick yourself up, have a nice cup of tea (of course!) and get back on track.

Author Preparation: Step 1

Practical exercise: Who are you writing your book for?

You are writing the book you wished you had read when you were going through the ups and downs on your journey. When you can see this, it makes it so much easier to know what to write as you are writing to yourself, but just a few years back.

Ask yourself these questions: What were the main challenges you were facing? What do you wish you had known back then? What would you have told yourself if you could go back in time? How did you want to feel?

Brainstorm these thoughts before moving onto the next step.

Author Preparation: Step 2

Practical exercise: Author Mission Statement

You are going to write an author mission statement that will set the positive intention of what you want to achieve with your book. Do not overthink the answers and if you feel your mission changes you can always come back and amend it. I will share my mission statement and then I will ask you some questions which will help you to write yours.

Author Mission Statement for *Share Your World*

I am writing a book for heart-led entrepreneurs, coaches and healers who want to share their story and create a positive difference in the world.

I will be sharing the practical tools and advice they need to become a respected author, combined with mindfulness tools which will empower them to release their past and recreate their future.

I am attracting authentic, heart-centred readers who are brave, fearless, and ready.

They will feel an instant energetic connection to my book which inspires them to take immediate action to make their dream of becoming an author reality.

Now it's your turn...

Clear your mind by listening to your author meditation before completing these sentences:

I am writing a book for…

I will be sharing…

I am attracting…

They will feel…

Let your words flow and trust that if your mission statement has a different format that's ok. No one else will ever have to read this.

Author preparation: Step 3

Practical exercise: A letter from your ideal reader

You are going to write a letter to yourself, from your ideal reader. This will help you to really get into the mind of your ideal reader, how they are feeling and the huge difference that your book has made to their life.

I will share the letter I wrote from my ideal reader and then I will ask you some questions which will help you to write yours.

A letter from my ideal reader for Share Your World

This is the actual letter I wrote from my ideal reader the day before I started to write this book.

Dear Cassandra,

I have just finished reading *Share Your World*. I knew from the very first page that your book was going to help me. My life has not gone to plan, it has been full of failure, disappointment and endless self-sabotage.

Like you I also felt I never fitted in, I have always shied away from the real me. I hid myself away in the shadows as I felt I was safe there, protected from the world and protected from the hurt. It didn't work, the more I hid the lonelier I felt. I have questioned so many times why my journey has been so crazy and what my purpose was.

I knew that the easy option was to stay in the dark, but was that what I really wanted in my life? I knew that there was a tiny spark within me that refused to go out and that it was my responsibility to re-ignite that spark. I decided that I could be sad, miserable and wallow in self-pity or I could do whatever it took to keep my flame burning so brightly that I would find my path and finally shine a light on the truth of who I am.

I knew that the only way back to finding myself was to allow myself to be the real me, with courage and without fear. I began my own personal development journey and felt like a weight had been lifted from my shoulders as I started to see life through new optimistic eyes.

There is a little voice inside my head saying, "You should write a book." I have replied to the voice telling it that I had no idea where to start, it just felt like a faraway dream. Despite wanting to share my journey I am quite a private person, I also have the tendency to overthink everything.

Surely little old me could never be a respected and renowned author? I am embarrassed to admit that I made up many excuses for not taking action as I was scared. I convinced myself that I would write my book one day, when the time was right. That was until I walked into Waterstone's and saw your book *Share Your World* right there in front of me.

I took one look at your beautiful cover and instantly knew this was the guidance I needed. Never in a million years did I think I could become a real author. I now know I can borrow your belief in me until I fully believe in myself.

I have been following your simple author preparation steps and I am astounded at how easily my words are flowing out, it's like you have tapped into a secret creative force within me! I love starting the day with your meditation and have a constant spring in my step which is rippling out into my business as well as every area of my life.

I have got no idea where you found your courage, strength and determination to keep going despite all of your challenges, but from the bottom of my heart thank you so much Cassie. You are the reason that I will now go on to fulfil my purpose, give my life meaning and become the woman I was born to be.

Your book has changed my life.

From your ideal reader x

Now it's your turn...

Listen to your meditation first to clear your mind and then begin to write from your heart, it may surprise you what comes out but just go with it. Remember back to how you felt when you were going through your challenges, imagine how amazing it would have felt to have discovered a relatable and non-judgemental book that you knew would help you to get your life back on track.

Could you see from my letter that my ideal reader is on a very similar path in life to me? She is just a few steps behind. This will be same with yours.

You can always come back and change it later if need be.

1) Start your letter by sharing how excited she was to have read your book. What did she love the most?

2) What are the challenges and struggles that were keeping her stuck? How were they feeling?

3) How has your book helped her to move forward with her life? Share how she feels now.

4) Finish by sharing the positive impact your book has had on her life and how you have played an important part in that.

I want you to write from your heart and connect emotionally with your letter so be prepared for a few tears as you write this. I welled up with tears when I wrote the last paragraph of mine (where are my emergency tissues?!) I see this as a positive sign that I am being pulled by my heartstrings to make sure that I make this commitment and finish what I've started. I know that you feel the same once you've written yours.

Author preparation: Step 4

Practical exercise: Dedication

You are going to write the dedication that will appear at the start of your book. My first two books were dedicated to my children. You will have already read my dedication for *Share Your World* at the start of this book, so here is the dedication from my first book.

Dedication from *The Girl Who Refused to Quit.*

For Kieron & Lennie. You always have been and always will be, my inspiration never to give up. Xx

Now it's your turn…

You may like to dedicate your book to your grandparents, parents, children, best friend, a teacher who always believed in you. Your book can be dedicated to anyone who has played an important part in your journey. Once again writing your dedication may evoke some emotion and that's ok.

Author preparation: Step 5

Practical exercise: Author playlist

You are going to make an 'I can do this!' playlist. Music is a very simple but very effective way to maintain your positivity and will also help to raise your energy before you write. Think back to when you have experienced challenging times in your life, what were the songs that helped you to get through the dark days? What were the songs that you felt empowered by? What song if it came on the radio right now would you have to stop what you are doing and strut your stuff to?

Here are a few of my favourites:

This is Me: Keala Settle

Voice Within: Christina Aguilera

Read All About It: Emeli Sandé

Wonder: Emeli Sandé

Rise Up: Andra Day

One Moment in Time: Whitney Houston

Girl on Fire: Alicia Keyes

I Am What I Am: Gloria Gaynor

I want you to listen to your playlist as often as you can, daily is best. I will often play mine as I'm making breakfast and getting ready for the day.

You can take this one step further by closing your eyes and imagining you can hear the songs playing at your book launch. Who will be there? What will you be wearing? Imagine holding your book and feeling so proud of yourself.

The power of writing to one person.

Have you ever listened to one of your favourite songs and felt like it was written especially for you?

I believe the reason for this is because the song writer has written the lyrics to just one person. They have vulnerably shared their deep and raw emotions. These songs have the power to move you to tears as they connect with you so strongly. This is exactly the same concept I want you to embrace when you begin to write your book.

You will be writing your book to just one person. You will be writing in a vulnerable way that shares your deep and raw emotions. Your book will have the power to move your ideal reader to tears as they connect with you so strongly. They will feel like you have written your book especially for them.

I will be sharing more advice on this topic later in the book but for now I want you to hold the thought of how powerful it is, when you just write to one person.

Author Tip You can also listen to your playlist whilst driving.

You now know my proven author preparation steps which will powerfully connect you to your goal of becoming a respected author. Following all of these steps will ensure that you stay determined, focused and motivated, even when the going gets tough.

Real life results

I am going to be sharing one of my *Share Your World* mentoring client's experience throughout the book.

I am very proud to share that Jacqueline E Rogerson has now published her first book *Onward and Upward* which is now available on Amazon. I would like to thank Jacqueline for allowing me to share her experience of working together.

Jacqueline's testimonial:

"I have always known I would write a book one day, but with no real idea how it would evolve or whether it was even something anyone would want to read. The author preparation steps, as delivered so brilliantly by Cassandra, have given me the clarity and focus I need to push forward and actually begin, with the end goal in sight. I can't wait to get started, especially now I have my author playlist to spur me on when it gets tough."

You have now set a solid emotional foundation for your book, but how can you take this one step further and begin to release any negative thoughts, fears and doubts that are holding you back?

Find out in Chapter 4.

Chapter 4

Call off the pity party!

Have you ever read a non-fiction book where the author is talking about a certain person or situation from their past and it has left you feeling uncomfortable? In some books this awkward feeling can filter through the entire book.

Why is this?

I believe that either the author's current energy, emotions and state of mind are negative, or they are still holding onto stagnant energy from their past. We have all experienced situations that, if given a choice, we would have preferred not to of happened. They did happen, but they are now in your past. You have moved on from this experience, you have grown in strength and you are now writing a life-changing book to share your story in a way that uplifts and empowers others. This is not an opportunity to hold a public pity party. This is also not an opportunity to self-diagnose yourself with P.O.M syndrome (Poor Old Me!).

Keeping it real.

If you are fortunate enough to be writing your book from a log cabin nestled on the edge of a beautiful lake, then that is amazing! However, I'm guessing that realistically you will be writing your book from your home around your already very busy life. Life has a funny way of trying to throw you off track when you set long term goals, so it is imperative to keep your feelings, emotions and energy as positive as possible throughout your author journey.

I want you to look back now at the words in your author mission statement. If you are truly committed to achieving this, then you need to accept the responsibility to release any negative emotions from your past. You also need to keep your energy in the present moment as positive as you can.

Don't panic!

I know this may seem like a big task, but I want to reassure you that we are all a work in progress. Unfortunately, there is no magic formula for waking up every day wanting to dance with the unicorns whilst spreading love, light and sparkles to the world! I can't give you dancing unicorns, but I believe the tools I will be sharing are the next best thing.

Tipping the balance on negativity.

I want you to think of your head like a pair of old fashioned weighing scales with weights balanced on either side. Most people's weights are tipped downwards, with negativity. There are many reasons for this including our past experiences, pressure from our daily life, not to mention the not so positive influence from most of the media! If you are serious about wanting to make a positive change in your life, and more importantly in the lives of others, you must tip the balance into positivity.

As an author you must take responsibility for, and manage, your own emotional state. The practical benefits of this include helping you to remain determined, motivated and calm so that you finish your manuscript and always reach your word count. But more importantly when you release any trapped emotions this new positive energy will have a ripple effect that will flow into your writing. This doesn't mean that you won't be sharing any dark moments in your book, what it does mean is that the overall tone of your writing will remain positive and uplifting, which your readers will sense. You may be wondering how you turn a public pity party into a public positivity party? You'll be pleased to know I have two very powerful tools to share with you, both of which you can implement into your life immediately.

The first tool is going to raise your self-awareness so that you can manage your emotions and increase your positivity on a day to day basis. The second tool will help you to release your negative emotions on a deeper level helping to shift any limiting beliefs that may have been with you for longer.

Tool 1 - Rate Your State

This tool is something I started using when my life collapsed for the third time in 2016. I refused to allow my external circumstances to govern my internal state of mind. It enables you not only to recognise your 'dark dips', but also helps you to quickly shift the way you feel.

Step 1: The first step is to 'Rate your State'. Each day I would check in with myself on a scale of 0-10 and rate how I felt.

I didn't have anything written down or an official chart of what each number equated to but here is an idea of the two extremes.

0 = Today I won't be getting dressed. I will be in bed, the duvet will remain over my head, possibly accompanied by tears streaming down my face and snot streaming from my nose.

10 = Today I will be dressed wearing full make up, hair curled, drinking frothy cappuccinos

accompanied by unicorn shaped chocolate sprinkles. I will gallop around my garden on my unicorn, spreading love, light and sparkles to the world!

Ok, so I may have slightly exaggerated my actions of a '10' day (because I don't drink caffeine!) but you get the picture. This a day when you bounce out of bed, everything is going to plan, life feels amazing, and you feel unstoppable.

Based on those two extremes ask yourself, 'What is my number?' There is no right or wrong. I have intentionally not filled in the definitions of the remaining numbers of 1-9 because this number is your perception of how you feel.

Step 2: The second step is to think about one thing you can do to reach just one number higher. That's right, just one number. The problem a lot of people encounter is that when they feel like a 2, they get annoyed and frustrated with themselves and will do one of two things. They either don't take any action, so they quickly end up sinking lower to a 1 or a 0, or, they get so annoyed and frustrated that they make a great master plan of how they are going to reach a number 10. I am all for taking responsibility for your feelings but it's not realistic to go from a 2 to a 10 in quick succession. Take the pressure off yourself and ask yourself what one thing can I do to get myself just one number higher? The amazing power of Rate

Your State this is that if you take action and know you can get yourself from a 3 to a 4 then you also have the power to take yourself from a 4 to a 5… and so on.

Here's the secret, don't aim for a 10! Yes, a 10 day is amazing, we all love those days when our superhero cape is flapping behind us, and we feel unstoppable, but it's not realistic to sustain this longer term. For me a 7 is an amazing place to be, but again you decide what feels good for you.

How can you increase your number?

Step 1: Ask yourself how would you like to feel? Happy, calm, relaxed, free, content, peaceful, joyful or hassle-free? (Or all of the above!?)

Step 2: Ask yourself what you can do to create that feeling? The trick here is the simpler the better.

Step 3: Make a list of anything and everything that makes you feel happy, calm, relaxed etc and keep adding to your list every time you think of something new. There is no right or wrong here, I will share an extract from my list below.

My feel-good list:

Music and dancing: I listen to songs which make me feel good, turn them up loud and dance. I'm not talking about step together step together boring kind of dancing, I'm talking strut your stuff like no one is watching kind of dancing! I also listen to powerful songs when I need to dig deep for belief and strength in myself.

Calming music: If I feel myself getting worried about something, listening to classical music can quickly calm me down. *Walking through Clouds* by Bernward Koch is an album I love (available from Amazon and all good music shops).

Talking: The 24/7 world of 'social' media can, ironically, leave us feeling very disconnected and alone as it can minimise the amount of real-life conversations we have. I make sure I pick up the phone and speak to a friend or arrange to meet up for a cup of tea and a chat so I have something to look forward to.

Walking: No matter how rubbish I feel and how unmotivated I am to leave the house, going for a walk always helps. It doesn't matter if it's ten minutes or an hour, it always helps to get some fresh air in my lungs and a fresh perspective on life. I will make eye contact and smile at anyone I pass and if this is reciprocated we will say 'hello' or 'good morning'. Yes, shock, horror I just admitted that I do talk to strangers! Humans crave interaction and just that small act of a smile can make the difference to someone else's day.

Getting outdoors: If it's not possible to go for a walk, just going out into my garden helps me feel better. If it's cold I'll wrap up warm and drink a cup of tea, if it's warm I'll sit, and have a cold drink or sometimes just walk around in bare feet on the grass.

Having fun: I enjoy simple activities like going to the park, playing on the swings, going down a slide, going on a boat trip, eating ice cream and having a picnic. They all bring back happy memories of being a carefree child. You don't have to have children to take part!

Sleeping: Although sleeping can't fix problems or change situations, I know that if I am exhausted and sleep deprived then going to bed at a reasonable time at night or having a power nap in the day can help to recharge my energy.

Now it's your turn...

What will you include on your feel-good list? It may be something that you used to do but just stopped due to life becoming busy.

Author Tip Write your list down and keep adding to it every time you think of something new.

The majority of the activities on my list are free or cost a very small amount of money. You may have activities that cost more money like going for a swim, joining a yoga class or booking a hair appointment, and that's ok too, it's whatever feels good for you.

When you read through your feel-good list you may be surprised to see that you are already doing some of these, but I'm guessing you only do them when you feel good. The secret to staying at a 5 or above is not just doing your feel-good list when you're feeling good, do it as often as you can. Check your number daily and if you do slip, it will drastically increase the speed at which you catch yourself falling and this will help you to climb back up quicker. As your number increases so will your energy and positive emotions which is good news for you and great news for your readers!

If you are a 5 of below my advice is not to write, concentrate on your feel-good list and once you are back up to a 6 or above you can pick your pen up again.

Tool 2 - Meditation

You hold the power!

You already have the most powerful source of creativity within you. Your inner guidance, your inner voice, your soul (whatever name you choose to give it) already knows what it wants to write. Your book is within you, the biggest challenge is cutting through the many layers of negative thoughts and beliefs you have accumulated over the years. Once you begin to release these layers you will not only tap into this unlimited source of creativity, but you will be brave enough to find the courage to share it.

How can you access this power?

Meditation acts to bypass your conscious mind, allowing direct communication with your subconscious mind.

"When you achieve a state of meditation, you unlock the door to your subconscious mind. That is where your power to create the life you deserve lives."

-Adrian Calbrese

I want you to now re-read that quote above by Adrian Calbrese.

If you haven't already done so I want you to commit to listening to your author meditation every single day. Did you just raise your eyebrows and make a face that said "Really?!" If so, I'd like you to re-read Adrian's quote above for the third time, haha!

I have previously mentioned that I don't, unfortunately, have a magic wand however I do believe that meditation is the next best thing. Once you commit to meditating on a daily basis you will quickly begin to feel the difference it brings to you and your life, in just 5 minutes a day! It's not the actual meditation that brings you this new perceived superpower, it's the positive feelings and emotions that the meditation evokes and leaves you with.

I believe meditation has the power to change people's lives. But if it's so simple and so powerful why don't more people do it?

Reasons why you may dislike meditation;

1) You are fed up of being asked to count backwards from 100 as you sit under your special tree, feel the wind in your hair and balance your root chakra!

2) You may get bored and impatient listening to the really loooooooong and boring introduction and being told how to breathe whilst sitting up straight with your legs crossed.

3) You feel frustrated when you are told to conjure up a completely unrealistic made-up scenario. Instead of feeling relaxed you may feel like screaming, "This is not real life!"

4) The stranger whose voice is meant to be calming you down is irritating you as they speak in a very monotone, very serious and very stern voice. Surely, they don't really speak like that!?

5) The music that accompanies the stranger's voice is boring and dull, or worse still there is no music.

6) The length of the overall meditation is far too long. If you do manage to make it to the end (calmly sealing yourself in a bubble of golden light!) you don't feel any different to when you started. Well, maybe irritated that you've just wasted half an hour!

Ways you might be persuaded to love meditation:

Research* shows that meditation:

1) Increases positive emotions.

2) Increases life satisfaction.

3) Boots your immune function.

4) Decreases pain.

5) Decreases inflammation.

6) Increases memory.

7) Improves attention.

8) Increases social connection.

9) Reduces loneliness.

10) Increases cortical thickness in your brain, especially in areas related to introspection and attention.

11) Increases grey matter in areas related to memory (hippocampus) and thought (frontal areas).

12) Increases brain volume specifically in areas for emotion regulation, positive emotions and self-control.

13) Decreases anxiety.

14) Decreases stress.

15) Decreases depression.

*This is a summary of an article in *Psychology Today*, written by Emma Seppälä PhD, on '20 Science-based reasons to start meditating today' where you can find the direct sources quoted.

www.emmaseppala.com/20-scientific-reasons-to-startmeditating-today.

A real-life story

I want to take you back to the summer of 2012 when my life had collapsed for the second time. I had dragged myself along to a mindset training day in the hope of rediscovering some of the pieces of my motivation (which had been missing in action for far too long).

That day I met a man who helped me to change my life, Dave O'Connor. As I sat in the audience I was glued to his every word, I wasn't in a very good place in my head but everything Dave said made so much sense. Suddenly, I found a glimmer of hope that I could turn my life around. As soon as Dave spoke about working together on a one to one basis I knew I had to invest in myself and he was the man who was going to help me. It was one of those moments when I couldn't afford to work with Dave, but I also couldn't afford not to work with him. I remember on our first call I said to him, "No pressure, Dave, but this is make or break."

We would have a coaching call and then Dave would make me a personalised meditation (a blueprint as he called it). Until this time, I had never found a meditation that I had liked, let alone listened to more than once. His meditations were so powerful that I would often cry listening to them, happy tears by the way. It was the combination of hearing my personal goals and how I wanted to feel, along with a familiar voice that I trusted and the beautiful background music that led to a very powerful transformation. This was at a time in my life when I could have easily given up on everything.

It was working with Dave that gave me a very powerful insight. The first time my life collapsed I was in a complete mess and I self-destructed. The second time my life collapsed I could have been a much bigger mess, but I realised that despite all the external chaos, my mind was extremely calm and piece by piece I managed to rebuild my life. I know that without a shadow of a doubt listening daily to these personal meditations that Dave made for me played a huge part in this.

Fast forward 6 months, and against all the odds I had set up my own business making bespoke meditations for women to help restore their body confidence. I will never forget the first one I made, sat in my kitchen nervously recording on a Dictaphone whilst playing the background music on my laptop! Some of my friends were personal trainers who kindly allowed me to work with their clients so that I could receive some testimonials. The amazing results of my work shocked the trainers and the clients, but no one was more surprised than I was when the testimonials came in a few weeks later!

What had I done?

I was inspired to scrap the traditional meditation rules and committed to making real meditations for real transformations.

1) There is no counting backwards, wind blowing in your hair or balancing of chakras. Personally, I love a bit of spirituality, so much so that I am now a very proud Reiki Master, but I like my meditations to be real.

2) The introduction is never any longer than 10 seconds and will never insist you sit up straight with your hands on your lap or sit crossed legged. Most

of the time I meditate I am curled up on my sofa with a cosy blanket over me.

3) I have a one-hour Skype call with my client to establish exactly what it is they are hoping to achieve and how they want to feel.

4) I use their name in the meditation - this is extremely powerful.

5) Having searched for three days, I record my meditations with the most beautiful, calming and uplifting music I could find.

6) Each meditation never lasts for any longer than five minutes.

Over the last five years I have continued to develop my meditations and believe that this is one of the most important parts of your author journey. I believe that life-changing books are written from the inside out, meditating daily is the quickest way to achieve this.

You'll be pleased to know I binned the Dictaphone and now use more sophisticated recording software!

The reason my meditations can be so powerful in less than 5 minutes is that they connect on a deep emotional level, which is exactly what you are also achieving by following my author preparation steps.

Real life results

I have made a beautiful bespoke meditation as part of my author mentoring programme. I asked Jacqueline to share how she felt after listening to her meditation for the very first time.

Jacqueline's testimonial:

"I have just listened to the bespoke meditation for the first time. I know I can do this. I believe in what I'm working towards so much and every minute of that first meditation I felt myself smiling and tingling with positive energy. This is happening. I am an author!"

Top Tips for Meditation

*Set an alarm on your phone to remind yourself to listen at least once a day.

*For best results listen once a day either first thing in the morning or last thing at night.

*Wear headphones when you listen, I have no scientific evidence, but it definitely makes it feel a lot more powerful.

*Never listen to a meditation when driving or operating machinery.

Here is the link for your free author meditation: Visit **www.cassandrafarren.com/free-meditations** and scroll down to the *Share Your World* meditation.

There is a very good chance that when you write your book, emotions from your past will rise to the surface. I see this as a positive experience as you are then in a position to heal and release them. I believe that writing a powerful book that will change the lives of others is 70% mindset and healing and only 30% writing. This is why the majority of my book is focused on attaining a positive mindset and encouraging you to take responsibility for, and increasing, your emotional resilience. This is why your words will flow out with ease once you have used my tools and mastered your mindset.

I want to congratulate you on being over halfway through my book now. I am guessing you are raring to pick your pen up and get writing.

Are we nearly there yet? Find out in Chapter 5.

Chapter 5

Are we nearly there yet?

Are you feeling like an excited child on a car journey who cannot wait to reach their destination!? I can reassure you that, yes, we are nearly there and no, it won't be long before you can finally put pen to paper and begin writing your book. I promise that every single part of this preparation will make your writing so much easier, as well as enjoyable. You do not need to become a stress head in the process, in fact the ladies I'm currently mentoring have all said they are feeling much happier and fulfilled since they have begun writing their book. It can be the same for you.

Are you ready to;

*Create the perfect emotional space which will allow your words to flow out with ease and reduce the risk of writer's block?

*Create the perfect physical space which will set the scene for a calm and enjoyable writing experience?

Excellent. Before we continue on our journey, I need to ask you a question, does anybody need to go to the toilet?! Sorry, I temporarily slipped into mum mode!

I have now reengaged my brain and will share my book writing endurance tips with you.

On your marks!

If you were planning on running a marathon, to have the best chance of completing the race it would be wise to plan well in advance of turning up on the starting line. The same guidelines apply to writing your book. Like running a marathon, writing and publishing your book is a long-term project that requires serious commitment and dedication. For complete transparency I want to make it clear that I have never run a marathon. The only time I would run is if I was being chased by a monster, or if the ice cream man was beginning to drive off down the street, obviously!

It's time to hibernate!

I believe we all underestimate how much negativity we are continually surrounded by. In our everyday lives it can be challenging to stay positive but when you are writing your book this is even more important. I am aware that it is unrealistic to take yourself on a writing retreat and come back to real life once you have a book in your hand. I am going to tell you how it is possible to have a mini retreat, without leaving your home. Does that sound good?

Here are some tips that will help you.

1) Hibernate from social media.

Now before you all shout at your book/screen I want you to hear me out. I don't mean that you must eliminate social media from your life completely, but what I do want you to realise is a) how much time you are wasting on there (which can turn into quality writing time) and b) how much negativity you are subconsciously absorbing, without even realising. I would recommend that one hour a day is plenty of time for your social media fix. I would encourage you to reduce the amount of time you spend aimlessly scrolling through your newsfeed and instead choose to use your time to contribute in positive and uplifting groups. I also recommend having a social media cut-off time when you turn the wi-fi off on your phone so that you can experience quality time to relax in the evening. The world will keep on turning even if you choose not to check your notifications for a few hours, pinkie promise!

A real-life story

One year ago, I deleted all the social media apps and e-mail accounts from my phone. I realised that it was constantly beeping with notifications which didn't feel good for my head, not to mention setting a bad example to my children. I didn't want them to grow up thinking that it was normal to have your phone glued to your hand or that it should ever be more important than the people you are spending time with. Yes, it did feel strange at first, but it wasn't until the constant noise and distraction had stopped that I realised just how much precious space it had been taking up in my head. I was still active on social media, it just meant that I had to log into my accounts from my laptop. I am often asked, how I do I stay so calm, positive and proactive, even when challenges occur? Having spent many years picking myself up from rock bottom I am now fiercely protective of what goes into my head and I would encourage you to embrace the same attitude.

2) Hibernate from the news.

The news is said to be one of the biggest negative influences in our lives. I haven't owned a television for over two years and I have chosen not to watch the news for a very long time. Some people may feel this strange and that I should know what's going on in the world. Believe me, the important news still finds you even if you don't infiltrate your brain by watching it first thing in the morning and last thing at night. I prefer to keep my mind as clear and as positive as possible so that I can make a difference to as many people's lives as I can. I would recommend that whilst writing your book you consider reducing watching and reading the news and focus on feeding your mind with positive influences instead.

3) Hibernate from negative people

It doesn't matter how excited you are about writing your book there will always be someone who wants to piss on your parade! There are many reasons that some people will not be as supportive as you may have hoped. My advice is to put your book writing blinkers on and keep your eyes on your goal. It is not always possible to eliminate these people from your life completely, but chances are it is possible to reduce the amount of time you spend with them. I would also be cautious about how much of your book writing journey you share with them. If they ask how it's going, a short and sweet positive answer before changing the topic is completely acceptable.

It makes me sad that I am even having to write about this, but I wanted to let you know that I have experienced the book 'neg heads' and that it is completely normal. There is a very good chance that they will be genuinely interested once you have accomplished your goal and have your book in your hand but until then I want you to remember this.

"Some will, some won't, so what!?"

This is a quote I learnt when I worked in network marketing and I believe it is as true in life as it is for book writing!

You don't need anyone else's approval to become an author and you certainly do not need to allow their fears and their doubts to stop you from reaching your goal.

By following these simple guidelines your mind will have a mini retreat as well as preparing that all important emotional space in your mind.

Get set!

You don't have to do it on the table! In fact, you can do it on your sofa, your bed, or even in the garden if you want to! I am talking about where to write your book from, of course!

A real-life example

With my first book I sat on the same chair in the same position at my kitchen table to write my entire manuscript. I found that with my second book I much preferred writing whilst sitting on my sofa or in my garden. The first 1728 words of this chapter were written on my bed and I have now moved downstairs to have a cup of tea before writing the rest from my sofa, as I'm a bit wild like that!

Try writing in different rooms and see what works best for you. It goes without saying that you will write much better if you are somewhere you will not be distracted.

Setting the scene.

This is my ideal way to prepare before I begin writing.

1) I will go for a walk, depending on how much time I have this can be vary from ten minutes up to one hour.

2) I will come home and listen to up to three songs from my author play list whilst preparing my writing treats (I will share more about these in a moment).

3) I will light a scented candle and ask myself, 'what do I want to write about today?' before listening to my meditation.

4) I will ensure my treats are within reach. These are a selection of food and drink that I look forward to consuming whilst writing. This helps to build a positive association each time I write. Here are a few of my favourites; Teapigs tea bags (peppermint and liquorice or lemon and ginger) Volvic lemon and lime water, fresh fruit, dried fruit and Haribo strawbs. Before the sugar police come and hunt me down I am not condoning eating an entire bag of

sweets every time you write, they are treats, so everything in moderation!

This preparation routine works well for me and I always look forward to writing.

Now it's your turn…

What will you include in your writing preparation routine?

Find out what works for you, but definitely listen to your meditation before writing as this will help to clear any negative thoughts and open up your creativity.

Real life results

Jacqueline's testimonial:

"I can't wait to start my writing each day, it's like 'me time' only better! I allow myself the time to be perfectly me and indulge in all the lovely things that make it so."

My writing routine.

Once I have completed my writing preparation it is time to start. I will be sharing in Chapter 6 how to plan the outline for your book so that you always know what to write, but until then I will share how I write so that you reduce the risk of experiencing writer's block, feeling overwhelmed or feel bored when writing.

1) I begin to play some relaxing music very quietly through my headphones and write for 45 minutes. The music and headphones are really important as I find they help to block out my cheeky little voice that tries to escape from my brain. You know the one I mean, it's like when I knew the first words in this book were going to be 'Once upon a time' my cheeky voice said, "You cannot write that!" I laughed and carried on regardless. The headphones won't stop the cheeky voice completely, but it most definitely helps.

You do not need to worry about finding the right words as you already have the most powerful source of creativity within you. I want you to write your book from your heart, and in order for this to happen I need you to trust yourself to speak out of a different body part, your words need to flow out of your heart and straight to your fingers. If you are questioning whether it is possible to speak out of a different body part I want you to ask yourself this; do you know anyone who speaks straight out of their arse!? Oh, my goodness, I can't believe I just wrote that, but I am not going to delete it to prove that I take my own advice, haha! My cheeky voice is saying to me now, "You can't include that!" My heart and fingers replied, "Oh yes we can!"

A real-life story

The music that I am listening to now is a beautiful compilation from YouTube called "The Best of Yiruma" I also listened to it on repeat whilst writing *Rule Your World*. It has currently been played 1,174,153 times and I wouldn't be surprised if the 174,153 of these were all down to me! I was in a restaurant having dinner with my family last month where they were playing Yiruma. Kieron, my eldest son, said to me, "Mum, this is your writing music!"

If at any point you feel you can't find the right words, stop what you are doing, close your eyes put your hand on your heart and ask yourself, "what do I want to say?"

2) After 45 minutes I make myself stop writing for 15 minutes. I then get up and do something completely different like put the washing away, do the washing up, vacuum a room or get another drink before coming back and starting to write for another 45 minutes.

This may seem completely random but as your brain knows you can get up and do something else after 45 minutes you don't feel guilty for giving yourself permission to sit and write. I find this works well as it gives my brain enough time to focus before having a break and I feel refreshed to come back and write again. I feel it is much more important to write 45 minutes' worth of quality work rather than forcing yourself to do three solid hours that will need a lot of editing.

I will mention at this point the importance of saving your work as you go. I would highly recommend you save it to a USB stick and to a cloud system such as Dropbox as it is heart-breaking to lose your hard work, I am talking from experience!

3) Once I have written my work I do not read back through it on the same day. This was a mistake I made with *The Girl Who Refused to Quit,* and I feel this one of the reasons it took me a lot longer to write it as I would read over it time and time again. Reading with a fresh pair of eyes the next day has reduced the amount of changes that I make to my work and dramatically increased the speed at which I write books.

In the publishing industry they have a term for you first draft, known as your 'Shitty First Draft!' This does not mean that your first draft has to be shit! What it does mean is that you can write your first draft whilst giving yourself the permission not to care too much about grammar and punctuation. My advice is always just to get writing! No one has to read a single word until you are ready to share your work.

4) The following day when I sit down to go through yesterday's work I read it through once in my head and then once out loud as I find this really helps to hear the flow of the words.

As with my writing preparation routine you do not have to follow these steps exactly, but this has been tried and tested. Who knew you could write a life-changing book and have a super tidy house at the same time!?

How many words should I write?

I don't follow the traditional publishing rules when it comes to word counts. I write books to give my readers transformation, not needless information.

I write the no-fluff version of exactly what they need to read. I do not write for the sake of it or just to make my book bigger. This week I had a call with an amazing aspiring author, Kelly Harris. Kelly asked me how long her book should be. I told her that on average a traditional book publisher would ask you to aim for approximately 40,000 words. I told her that all of my books are approximately 25,000 words and that whilst I don't feel it should be any less than this I believe that when you're done you're done.

Kelly's book is about the journey of grief through a mother's eyes which will support parents who have experienced the loss of a child. I asked if her ideal reader would want to read a long book? She answered honestly that it was highly unlikely that they would even pick a book up if it was too long.

Let's say a normal non-fiction book may take you three hours to read and one of my books took you one and a half hours, I would much rather you finish my book and then use the other hour and a half to implement the knowledge you have learned. Acquiring knowledge is a complete waste of time unless you use it. Take yourself into the metaphorical shoes of your ideal reader. Do they really want to pick up and read a huge book? If you are self-publishing, then always remember that you are writing your book on your terms.

A real-life story

When I was having the cover designed for *Rule Your World* I found out that due to it being shorter than the average book I was unable to have the title written down the spine of the book. I was a bit disheartened when I found out but then reminded myself of one of my favourite quotes, 'It's what's on the inside that matters'.

The first comment I often get when I show my book with anyone is this, "I love how small it is!" nobody has ever said, "I was interested in buying your book

Cassandra, but since it doesn't have the title on the spine I've changed my mind!"

Write from your heart, share your message and remember when you're done your done.

Go!

If you are still wondering, "Are we nearly there yet?" Yes, we are!

You may now to proceed to Chapter 6 where you finally get to the exciting part you have been patiently waiting for!

Chapter 6

Pick your pen up!

So here we are, we have finally arrived at the part where you can begin to take action. But before you start writing it's important to make a plan. Having an outline for your book will make it so much easier to know what to write and to make sure your book's message comes across loud and clear.

At this point I feel it's important to share with you the difference between an autobiography and a memoir.

An autobiography focuses on the chronology of the writer's entire life e.g. from childhood (birthplace, childhood memories and education) to adulthood (relationships, career and family life) and beyond.

A memoir, which your book will be, is a collection of memories that have had a profound impact on the author's life. They aren't necessarily shared chronologically.

A memoir reveals the feelings of the author and focuses more on their experience of an event rather than the actual event itself. A memoir often has deeper meaning as it also shares what has been learnt as a result of their experience.

I want to share a little secret with you, your memoir is not about you. You will be sharing a collection of memories that have had a profound effect on your life, but your book is not about you. The purpose of sharing these memories and their accompanying feelings and emotions is to give your ideal reader the insights and space to reflect so they can apply the message and the meaning from your book into their own life.

Where does your story begin?

You might be wondering about how to start your story. If I don't start writing my book from the beginning of my life, where do I begin?

Practical exercise

Take a moment to think back over your collection of memories, particularly those which had a big impact on your life. I want you to ask yourself what was the most profound moment when everything changed? If this moment doesn't come to you immediately listen to some relaxing music, close your eyes, put your hand on your heart and ask yourself, "Where does my story begin?" Trust the answer that comes to you and write this down in your journal.

A real-life story

Over five years ago I took a deep breath and intuitively wrote the very first words of my memoir which were, 'I couldn't breathe.' I'll be honest I didn't have an outline for my book, as at this point I wasn't aware it was going to become a book, but I remember just knowing that was where my story began, that was when everything in my life had changed. I have since spoken to many people who have told me they were hooked on reading my book from the first few words.

Trust your instincts. You already have this knowledge within you. It may not seem like the most logical place to start but remember that you are writing your book from your heart, not from your head.

Practical exercise

What is your message?

Go back to your author preparation steps where you wrote a letter to your ideal reader. I want you to read this again and really hold the vision of your ideal reader in your mind.

I want you to imagine that you open your front door and see your ideal reader stood in front of you. If you only had 10 seconds to give her one encouraging message before the door closes and you never see her again, what would you shout?

Your answer is your overall message and the purpose of your book. Write this down in your journal.

A real-life example

Jacqueline would shout, "You always have a choice."

Once you have your overall message this forms a metaphorical umbrella over all of the memories you will share. They will all in some way relate to this message. Once you have discovered your message you are ready to start planning the outline of your book.

Practical exercise

How to plan the outline of your book;

1) You will need a large piece of paper, ideally A4 or bigger.
2) Turn the paper horizontally and write your overall message and purpose of your book across the top of the paper.
3) Draw a straight line that goes all the way across the page, in the middle of the paper.
4) The furthest point on the left-hand side is where your story begins, the furthest point on the right-

    hand side is where your story ends (e.g. where your life is now).

5) I want you to think back over your memories along this timeline and identify between 10 to 12 key moments/stories in your life that all fall under the core message of your book.

6) Identify whether this is a light memory, getting a new job, starting a new relationship etc or a dark memory of being made redundant, ending a relationship.

7) Plot these memories out along your timeline in chronological order. If it is a light memory write it above your timeline, if it is a dark memory write it below your timeline.

8) Each of these key moments will become a chapter of your book. To help you elaborate on what to include in each chapter take yourself back to each memory and brainstorm on your paper what happened at that time in your life. How did you feel, what did you learn? What were you proud of? What did you gain strength from? If you could go back in time what message or advice would you give yourself now?

9) As I previously mentioned if you have chosen to self-publish you are in control of your word count but if you aim for approximately 2500 words per chapter this will give you between 25,000 and 30,000 words for your book.

Keep your outline safe as you will need to refer back to this each time you write to help keep you on track.

Write naked!

It is emotion, not information, that will inspire your reader. She wants to know exactly how you were feeling in the moment of the memory you are sharing. This means that you have to write with an all-or-nothing attitude in a way that scares you a bit. You are (*hypothetically) writing naked!

Writing (*hypothetically) naked with an all-or-nothing attitude means you may feel vulnerable at times but when that emotional connection is made with the reader, that's when the magic happens.

It is worth saying at this point that even though I recommend (*hypothetically) writing naked you are in control of what you write at all times. You do not have to share anything you don't feel comfortable with. Until you send your first draft to your editor nobody else is going to read a single word.

P.S *Yes, I do feel the need to clarify that I'm not suggesting real life nakedness whilst you write as a) I may get sued if you get caught writing naked anywhere in public, and b) that's a bit weird!

The secret to writing a life-changing book.

Have you ever read a book that feels like a long boring lecture, written in such a generic tone that it could have been written by anyone for anyone? The secret to writing a powerful memoir is to form an emotional connection with your ideal reader and to write in a way that makes them feel like you have written your book especially for them. It can sometimes be challenging to form an emotional connection in a real-life conversation when you have feedback from the other person through non-verbal communication, so how can you form an emotional bond in a book when there is no two-way communication? Simple… you find your voice.

Who are you talking to?

You have written your mission statement and your letter to your ideal reader, now it's time to talk to her. I want you to imagine that your ideal reader has come to your house for a cup of tea and has asked you to share your story with her. I want you to write in **exactly** the same conversational way in which you would speak to her in real life. I don't want you to second guess yourself or mute your voice; all your little quirks that make you unique is exactly what she wants to hear. She wants to hear your story in your voice. Do not try to put on an 'author's voice' or anyone else's voice for that matter, this will only diminish your power.

Remember that your ideal reader is exactly like you, just a few years behind. Speak to her with kindness and compassion but do not hold back, she wants to know the truth and will respect you for writing in such a real and honest tone. This is what will set your book apart from any other author in the market. There will always be other authors who will be writing about similar experiences but no one in the world can write in your voice, be proud of who you are and speak your truth.

I'll be honest, it takes a lot of courage to write in a conversational tone. You have to hold your nerve and trust that the words that come out are the right ones. This is why is it is so important to follow all of the preparation steps so that by the time you write, you have turned down your naughty inner voice and turned up your confidence, so you can trust your voice. If there is a word or a sentence that you wouldn't say in real life, then definitely don't write it in your book.

A real-life example

This book could have been a boring, generic manual that just gave you the practical steps to follow to write your book. The main reason I hope you have found it enjoyable is that I have written my book as though I am speaking to you in real life.

When you follow these simple, but powerful, principles your ideal reader will feel like your book was written especially for her. You will find that your words flow easily and that sharing your memories are as simple as having a real-life conversation.

Author Tip

If at any point you feel stuck with your words place your hand on your heart and ask yourself out loud, "What do I want to say?" or "What am I trying to say?"

Share don't tell!

This book is called *Share Your World* for a reason. Your ideal reader wants you to share your memories in a way that she can relive them through you.

A real-life example

I am going to share with you the opening of *The Girl Who Refused to Quit;*

"I couldn't breathe. My legs felt like lead as I tried to climb the stairs. I couldn't fight it, the grief took over and my legs collapsed beneath me. I couldn't see for the tears that were streaming down my face as I sat sobbing halfway up the stairs. I knew from the physical pain I could feel in my heart that the last hour of my life had not been a dream but a living nightmare that was about to change my life as I knew it. Part of me wanted to scream and shout, the other part wanted to go to sleep and wake up when all the pain was gone. Would it ever go?"

I could have written;

"In April 2003 I unexpectedly became a single parent. I was shocked and upset. I cried a lot of tears that evening."

Can you see how much more powerful it is to share my experience with you rather than just telling you what happened?

Practical Exercise

Let's get writing!

1) I want you to go back to Chapter 5 and complete your writing preparation steps.

2) Look at your book outline and choose your first key memory to write about. I wrote mine in chronological order from my starting point as I found it flowed better, but you can decide the order in which you choose to write.

3) Once you have written your first key memory, of approximately 2500 words, that is your first chapter written!

4) Go to your next memory in the outline of your book and repeat this process. Share each memory as vividly you can. Always keep your ideal reader in mind as you write, it may help to imagine you are writing her a (very long) letter or sharing your diary/journal entries with her. This conversational tone is exactly what she wants to hear.

If you were to write 500 words every day for 60 days, you will be the very proud owner of a of 30,000-word manuscript! That's not a lot to ask, is it!? It's about the equivalent of writing a blog a day.

I told you it was simple.

Once you have written out all of your key memories, it's time to congratulate yourself because you've got the first draft of your manuscript ready!

Real-life results

"Working with Cassandra to begin writing my first book has been completely transformational. She has a wonderful way of making sure believing in yourself is top of the list and without this I am sure I would have struggled much more with self-doubt. Before we began working together I had some quite fluffy ideas about writing a book, but they remained as ideas in my head.

I am happy to say that not only have I now finished writing my first book, I have gained enough momentum to actually bring it to life in a publication."

Jacqueline E Rogerson. Author of *Onward and Upward* – now available from Amazon.

Remember, you do not need to have all the answers or to be exactly where you want to be in your life at the end of your timeline. You may wish to reflect on your journey or to look back at the lessons you have learnt but just sharing your experiences, memories and feelings in your true, authentic voice, is enough to write a life-changing book!

You should feel extremely proud of yourself once you have finished writing the first draft of your manuscript. However, your mind may be racing as you wonder what happens next.

How will this document turn into a real-life book? Where do you begin with marketing your book? And do you really have what it takes to see this through to the end and become a respected author?

Do not fear, Cassandra is here! All will be revealed in Chapter 7.

Author Tip

I highly recommend that you read this article by Helen Sedwick on how to use real people in your writing without ending up in court. There are a few simple rules you can follow to make sure you protect yourself.

http://helensedwick.com/how-to-use-real-people-in-your-writing/

Chapter 7

It's time to share your world!

I understand that this is the part where most authors feel apprehensive, but I want you to take a step back for a moment and realise that if you can find the courage and confidence to share your deepest, most intimate feelings and experiences by writing your first draft, then turning it into a book shouldn't be challenging. You have already done the hard bit!

I love a good analogy, one that I like comparing to writing a book is buying a house. When I worked as a mortgage adviser my customers would bounce into my office full of excitement, present me with a glossy brochure with their dream house on it and confidently say, "This is our new house!". The majority had no idea how long the process would take from their initial mortgage interview to receiving the keys to their new house. It didn't matter to them. They wanted the house so badly that they were prepared to take the next steps of paying for a valuation, receiving a mortgage offer, instructing a solicitor, getting searches done, signing and exchanging contracts as and when they needed to, until finally a few months later they would move into their dream house.

Just like the process of buying a house, publishing a book can feel overwhelming at times but remember that all you need to do is to take the next step. As with anything in life you can invest your own time and energy or if you would prefer an expert to relieve you of the pressure, there are a wealth of experts and self-publishing companies who you can pay to make the process quicker and easier.

If you have chosen to traditionally publish, your publishing house will have a team of experts who complete these next steps on your behalf.

Do you have a book title?

If you haven't already decided on a title for your book, now is a good time.

It has been said that shorter titles work better and that three-word titles are ideal but as I have said from the start, this is your book on your terms. I didn't follow the rules with my slightly longer title of *The Girl Who Refused to Quit* but *Rule Your World* and *Share Your World* are both short and sweet.

Write the final pages for the inside of your book.

You will need;

A copyright page that asserts your rights as an author.

An author bio page, which tells the reader a bit about you.

An acknowledgements page and a dedication page (you have written this in Chapter 2!).

You may wish to have a table of contents/list of chapters and page numbers.

You may also wish to include a contact page at the end of the book.

The steps to self-publishing

Michelle Emerson from www.michelleemerson.co.uk is an author, experienced editor and self-publishing expert who I have worked with and highly recommend. I asked if she could share an overview of the next steps to take once the first draft of your manuscript is written. Here's what she told me:

You will need to have your book proofread and edited.

A proofreader and an editor are both responsible for ensuring your writing is accurately and professionally presented. However, there are substantial differences between the two. A proofreader will check your document for typos and spellings, as well as grammar and punctuation (as will an editor). But the editor will add an extra layer of digging, tweaking and upgrading.

Proofreading is the process of correcting surface errors in writing, such as grammatical, spelling, punctuation and other language mistakes.

Formatting your book for Kindle and/or typesetting your book for print

There are differences between the two so please don't assume that once you've formatted your book for Kindle that the print version will just be the same.

Decide on which publishing platform you want to use

There are a whole host of options here – I use Amazon KDP and/or CreateSpace for my authors' books, but you might want to investigate Ingram Spark or Lulu (do a Google search if you want to find out the entire range of self-publishing or print-on-demand companies).

Write your blurb/Amazon description

A blurb is the writing which appears on the back cover of a paperback and once you've created this you can tweak it to use as your Amazon description too. It needs to be pithy and punchy, simple to read, and don't give too much away (hooks are a great way to make people buy).

Research into keywords, categories & pricing

If you want your book to stand out (and not get swamped by the competition) invest time in researching the best keywords, categories and pricing bracket for your book. Which categories are the best-selling books in your niche sat in? What keywords do they use? How much are they selling their books for? Research time is time well spent if you want any kind of longevity (and sales).

ISBN numbers

An ISBN is an internationally-recognised number used by booksellers, libraries, publishers, internet retailers and other supply chain organisations for ordering, listing, sales records and stock control purposes. It identifies the owner/author as well as the book title, edition and format. Amazon KDP and CreateSpace will assign you a free ISBN number if you use their platforms to publish. If you use other print-on-demand companies, you will need to purchase your own ISBN number.

Design your cover

This is the fun part! It really does feel like a 'real book' once you can see the vision for you cover brought to life. Have a look on Amazon at other books in the "memoir" category and see which covers you like and which ones you don't. Are there any fonts or backgrounds that really jump out at you?

The person who said we don't judge a book by its cover wasn't telling the truth! Think back to the books that you have bought, and you will know that the cover plays a huge part in your decision of whether to buy or not to buy.

Quick tip from Cassandra

I would recommend that you pay a professional to design your cover. If your book looks cheap and basic it's unlikely your readers will feel compelled to get reading! Think about all the hours of work that you have dedicated to writing your story. You will be sharing your book for many years to come so I believe in making it the best it can be.

It is a good idea not to choose white as your background colour as if your book is listed on Amazon it will get lost within their white background.

If you are going to publish a paperback the back cover of your book also needs to look professional and be laid out correctly. Your book cover designer will work out the spine size of your book based on the number of pages in your book.

I recommend having your photograph on the back cover of your book as your readers want to see who the amazing author is. I would make this a professional photograph and not your favourite selfie. If you want to be taken seriously as an author, you need to look professional.

Back to Michelle

Create and set up Your Amazon KDP/CreateSpace/other accounts

As well as everything book-related you'll also need your bank details, and tax information (UTR number if you're in the UK) to hand during the set-up process.

Upload your book

Once everything is set up, you'll have to upload your e-book or PDF to your chosen platform and go through the proofing/review process to make sure it looks well presented.

Back to Cassandra

Final step = buy wine and celebrate!!

As I mentioned at the start of this chapter there are many businesses (including Michelle's) that can help you with every aspect of your self-publishing journey. There are also many online resources and books, which will elaborate on this information, if you would prefer to invest your time and achieve the results yourself.

Let's talk about marketing!

As with self-publishing, marketing is a huge topic that could warrant an entire book.

Before I begin I'd like to share some advice I was given when I published my first book.

"It's not a sprint, it's a marathon."

With a self-published book it is your responsibility to get your book in front of your ideal readers. Yes, it will most likely be available for sale on Amazon but it's less likely that your readers will randomly stumble across it.

15 Top Tips for Book Marketing

1) Share your journey: It is best to think about marketing early on in your author journey. It's true that you don't have a book to sell but there's nothing stopping you from building an audience of potential readers from the moment you commit to writing your book. A simple way to do this is through social media. You could share a post that says, "I've just read an amazing book called *Share Your World*, I'm so excited that I am finally going to become an author!" You could write a weekly post, sharing how many words you are up to or how you are loving the journey.

2) Create a Facebook group: Opening a group especially for your book has many benefits. After a month or so of sharing your weekly book updates you can open a group and message anyone who has liked or commented on your author updates. It's important that you always invite people to your group and don't just add them. A group is a great way to engage with your readers and build a buzz as you continue writing. You could share ideas for your title, cover design or even a sample of your book. You can add the group link in your book to encourage new readers to join; this is also a great way of getting feedback and asking readers to leave reviews once your book is published.

Real life results

This is Jacqueline's experience of setting up her Facebook group;

"I was so nervous about setting up my first Facebook group. No one will want to come, I thought. But I don't want to randomly add friends and family either, I need real supporters. So, I put a post that simply said if you are really interested in hearing more about my first book and its developments, please join here. Within a fortnight I had almost 50 members, and just 6 weeks later I now have 70.

They are my real-life fan club, my cheerleaders I call them, they give me fantastic feedback on the excerpts I have shared, are happy to comment on occasional errors too, they have helped me get the word out there about my book before it is finished and have had some insightful opinions about what I'm doing that just help me to know I need to keep doing it.

Having the group has truly been a wonderful experience, it's been a safe place to share the highs and lows of writing the book as well as somewhere that's always full of enthusiasm for my writing. I love it."

3) E-mail list: If you have an e-mail list send them regular interesting blogs with updates of your book and create a countdown to your publishing date.

4) Join Facebook groups: There are many Facebook groups specifically for authors. Join a few that have good engagement and always read the rules before posting. Make sure you post regularly to build relationships with other members and definitely don't overpromote your book.

5) Twitter: You can post regular updates on Twitter and use the hashtags #author #authorlife #amwriting #shareyourworld. There is also a hashtag you can use to find journalists looking to interview people for their articles #journorequest. There is no guarantee of being published but it's worth checking these on a regular basis.

6) PR: You may want to conquer the world by sharing your message but start in your own town. Do some research into your local newspapers and radio stations and find out how you can contact them to potentially get featured. It's worth noting they are not always that interested in the fact you have written a book, they are more interested in the story behind the book or how you will be using your book to make a positive difference.

If you are invited to speak always give as much value and advice to the listeners as possible, you're not there to sell. I have spoken on the radio eight times and the presenter has always mentioned my books and website at the end of the interview. Wear something you feel really good in and always ask for a photograph with the presenter as this can be shared on social media.

Author Tip I recently read and highly recommend 'Your Press Release is Breaking my Heart' written by Janet Murray. This is a practical guide on how to get your business featured in national newspapers, magazines and on radio and TV.

7) Local magazines: Do you have any local community magazines delivered to your house? They are often looking for features or may have a book review section. Pick up the phone, be polite and ask if they'd like to write a feature on your book.

8) Blogs and podcasts: As well as writing and sending out your own blogs you can build relationships with other like-minded business owners who are looking for guest bloggers. Always make sure you can add a link to your book in your bio and add your social media links so potential readers can contact you.

9) Local community: Research local cafes, groups and charities who may be interested in having your books on display. When I wrote *Rule Your World* I discovered there was a local 'Happiness Café' called

'Johnny's Happy Place' in my town. I turned up with a friendly smile, introduced myself and asked Denise, the manager, if she would be interested in displaying my books. They now have both of my books on every table, I've had amazing feedback saying how much their customers have enjoyed reading them. Denise gave me a direct phone number for a local journalist who then wrote a feature on our collaboration with the headline, "Author Cassie Finds Happiness" which certainly made me very happy!

10) Real life book launch: You can invite your friends, family, clients and readers to a launch where you celebrate the release of your book. You can have your books for sale and take the opportunity to sign copies for buyers and have your photo taken. Encourage your guests to share their photos of the event on social media. You could also livestream a video from your launch to share on social media.

11) Online book launch: I will admit that I felt more nervous holding an online book launch than a real life one! I added a new event on my Facebook page, invited guests who had followed my journey, poured myself a glass of wine (for the nerves!) and hoped for the best! I started by sharing the reasons behind why I had written the book and read a chapter out live. I was overwhelmed with how many people joined me live for support. It has since been viewed over 1.4k times, so it was definitely worth the initial nerves! I also ran a book giveaway where I asked the viewers to write in the comments "I'm ready to rule my world" and I announced the winner live the following week. It went so well that I continued to livestream "Cassanory" as it affectionately became known, every week for the next month. Each week sharing updates, answering questions and running a book giveaway at the end of each call. I built a regular group of viewers and was even messaged by one man requesting a shout out to his nan who loved my books and tuned in to watch "Cassanory" each week. Both of my children thought that very cool!

12) Local networking events: Attending local networking events will help you to build up trust and rapport with business owners who, even if they aren't your ideal reader, might know someone who is. I'm sure you wouldn't do this but never attend an event with a "selling" attitude. Get to know who is in the room, what they do and how you can help them. The majority of events have a guest speaker which is a great opportunity to speak about your book. I attended an event in October, put my name down on the guest speaker list and was advised it would be up to six months before there was a space. Two weeks later I received a phone call. They had a cancellation and asked if I wanted to speak at the next meeting, which was a week later (1st November) on the exact day of my book launch! My little voice cheekily tried to tell me that this wasn't much time to prepare a talk, but the voice came out of my mouth said, "I would love to, thank you!" Inspirational authors say, "yes", then figure out the way!

13) Speaking at events: This is a great way to raise your profile and to share your message on a larger scale. Event organisers like to book authors as they are seen as an authority. It also comes with the extra sales opportunity, if the audience enjoy your talk they can purchase a signed copy of your book after the event.

14) Always carry at least one copy of your book in your handbag! I have sold my books in some random places after I've been asked the question, "What do you do?" Once I share that I am an author they ask, "What books have you written?" I reach into my handbag and their eyes light up like I'm about to pull a rabbit out of a hat but (even more magical!) I pull my books out of my bag!

15) Call yourself an author: This may sound obvious, but I didn't call myself an author for a while after I had written my first book, I used to tell people that 'I had written a book' instead. When I look back it's a shame I didn't have that confidence.

Be proud of what you have achieved and own your author status. Update your business cards, website and social media platforms to say 'author' in addition to your current business and display the link to your book.

A real-life story

In January I received a message on LinkedIn from a company I had never connected with, asking me to submit a proposal to run two days 'training in Dubai before flying to Kuala Lumpur where they wanted me to deliver another training course. They had found my profile based on the fact I was an author who had written a book on emotional resilience.

The work didn't go ahead for several reasons, but I wanted to share this example to show how becoming an author automatically makes you an expert in your field of work.

Now that big chunk of, very relevant, logic is out there I can continue with the part that I feel extremely passionate about sharing with you.

What are you waiting for?

If you have read this far then congratulations!

*You have discovered why so many writers unnecessarily stay stuck in fear.

*You now know a powerful way to beat procrastination, so that nothing will stop you from finishing writing your book.

*You have found out my powerful, proven, author preparation steps which have connected you to your goal on a deep emotional level.

*You have discovered how to effortlessly release yourself from your past along with any trapped emotions you were holding onto, to ensure that the tone of your book remains upbeat and uplifting.

*You have learnt how to create the perfect emotional space which will always allow your words to flow with ease and eliminate writer's block.

*You have found out how to create the perfect physical space which will set the scene for a calm and enjoyable writing experience.

*You have discovered how to have the courage and confidence to find your voice which will set your book apart from other authors.

*You have found out how to write in such a powerful way that your readers will feel like your book was written especially for them.

*You have discovered my powerful technique to plan the outline of your chapters as well as discovering your overall message and purpose of your book.

*You have learnt how to remain consistently focused and motivated, so that at the end of 60 days you will be the proud owner of the first draft of your manuscript.

*You now know the next steps to publishing once the first draft of your manuscript is written.

* You now understand how to begin marketing your book to your ideal readers.

You now have a choice.

Option 1: You can put the book down, leave me a review on Amazon (they really do mean the world to me!) take no action and remain in the large percentage of people who are 'writing a book'. You can carry on with your life as you continue to wait for the right time to make a difference to the lives of others and become a respected and renowned author.

Option 2: You can put the book down, leave me a review on Amazon (if you don't ask you don't get!) and make the decision right here, right now, that you will do whatever it takes to finish writing your book. You commit to making a difference to the lives of others as you finish what you've started and proudly become a respected and renowned author.

Harsh but true

I will be completely honest with you, nobody cares if you don't write your book. Think about this for a moment, why would they? If you are going to make this happen you need an all-or-nothing, positive attitude. You need to carry this momentum forward and take action immediately.

The right time will never come.

Realistically it could take up to six months to write, publish and begin to market your book (which is still very quick!) I want you to think back over the last five years your life, has there ever been a period of six months that have been completely blissful without a single blip in your personal life or business? I am guessing that you have had many blips, some bigger than others, but if you are human then this is part of life. Would you also agree that reaching a point of no stress and complete serenity with no blips is highly unlikely for a six-month period of your life? So, would you also agree that there will never be the 'right' time to write your book?

I want to remind you of how alone, afraid and overwhelmed you felt in your darkest times. There is someone out there right now who is feeling the same. What would you have given to have read a relatable, non-judgemental book which gave you hope that you could begin to see the light at the end of the tunnel? Your ideal reader feels the same. She needs to read your book now, not when it conveniently fits into your future rose-tinted life. Have you ever read a book which had a massive profound impact on your life which came into your life at exactly the right time? How would your life be different now if the author decided they were going to wait for the right time to come before they could be bothered to share their book with you?

A real-life story

You will never forget seeing your book for the very first time. Holding it in your hands, feeling so proud to see your name on the front cover knowing that all your hard work was worth it is a moment you will treasure forever. You may even hear yourself say the words, "It's a real book!" as until then it is hard to imagine exactly how it will look and feel.

I was beaming with pride the day the first copy of *The Girl Who Refused to Quit* was delivered to my house. I remember seeing the delivery van pull into my street, I literally ran to my front door and stood on the driveway with a huge smile on my face to be greeted by a confused delivery man, with a strange look on his face! I explained that he had just delivered the first copy of my book, which turned his confusion into a smile as he told me he actually felt like he'd done something worthwhile in his job.

As he left, I stood with the cardboard box in my hands, shaking. Part of me wanted to rip it open quickly, but part of me was scared. This was it: my moment, my journey, my book – all neatly bubble-wrapped in a box. I slowly opened the package and held the book in my quivering hands. Wow!

There she was, *The Girl Who Refused to Quit,* ready to share her journey and hoping to inspire others with her story.

It had been two years since that life-changing phone call with Sandie who encouraged me to "begin writing down my journey" and that "everything would become apparent".

When I began to write *Rule Your World* I had a larger sense of urgency. From the moment my counsellor told me not to come back, as I had reached a point of acceptance on my own in just six weeks, I knew that my message had to be shared. This was after my life had unexpectedly collapsed and I had become a single parent for the third time in February 2016. However, at that moment I was faced with the huge upheaval of finding and moving to a new house. My priority was providing emotional and physical stability for my children.

It was a few months later in August 2016 when a friend said to me, "You do know you need to write a book to help others with what you've been through" and she was right. I did know but I had been putting it off as we got settled into our new house and our new life. I felt overwhelmed with doubts and questioned if I was the author's equivalent of a one-trick pony! Could I write a self-help book? Did I have enough content? Would anyone take me seriously writing about my experiential real-life lessons as opposed to studying eight degrees in the subject? I put my doubts to one side and I began to write.

Two weeks later I received a devastating phone call from my dad at 7am to say that my mum had gone missing and the police had been called. Thankfully my mum, who has Alzheimer's, was quickly found safe and well but unfortunately the emotional trauma of realising how bad her disease had got, lasted long after that awful morning she went missing. It completely threw my newly-settled life off kilter which had a knock-on effect on my business and income. I knew I didn't want to quit my business, but I needed to take the financial pressure off myself whilst I sorted my head out. Long story short I began working on a freelance basis for two companies. Unfortunately, the organisation who were paying a contribution towards my rent stopped this payment without any notice. I was advised to appeal the decision to get it reinstated. Three very long months later, after a lot of stress, tears and an exhausting fifty-hour week working as a temp to raise the money they claimed I owed, they finally agreed to reinstate the payment. It is safe to say that I had absolutely no inclination to continue with writing my book during this time.

In January 2017, I breathed a big sigh of relief. I knew that I wanted to get back on track with my business and to finally get my second book finished. Two weeks later my mum was rushed into hospital with multiple blood clots, we were told there was a good chance she wouldn't live. Somehow, she pulled through and made a miraculous recovery, but once again the stress affected me on a deeper level. I was ill for a few weeks after, and once again lost the momentum with my business and book. I spent the next few months taking small steps towards building up my business and my emotional strength.

On the 1st June 2017, I knew it was time to pick my pen up again, I had this overwhelming desire within me. I knew that I had to get my book finished, and quickly. I was still running my business, working two freelance jobs whilst working around school hours bringing up my children. I kept my focus, made sacrifices and I was so proud to publish my book just five months later on the 1st November 2017.

I had been feeling frustrated in the last month before it was published and lost confidence in my work. I remember joking to a few people that, "I wanted to put my manuscript in the bin". Be careful what you wish for as my considerate postman actually left the first delivery of my books safely in my recycling bin! Thankfully they were all intact (and didn't smell!) and once again I had that overwhelming feeling of pride as I took the first copy out of the box.

My mum and dad were due to arrive at my house later that afternoon, so I proudly signed the first copy for them and placed it on the table. A few hours later we were all standing in my kitchen as we laughed at how my books had ended up in the bin. I handed them their copy. My dad's face lit up as he told me how proud he was and how he loved the front cover. He then passed it to my mum who looked me straight in the eye and exclaimed, "Wow, this book looks amazing, did somebody give it to you?"

My mum was holding my book in her hand, yet she did not know that the author, her daughter, was stood in front of her. I walked out of the room with tears in my eyes, knowing that I would have to live with the painful regret of not writing my book fast enough. I wanted to make my mum proud, yet she never has and never will read *Rule Your World*.

Sadly, my mum's Alzheimer's has got increasingly worse. One month ago, only six weeks after I had started to write *Share Your World*, I collected my mum from the house she had lived in for over 30 years. I took her out to lunch and we went for a lovely walk at one of our favourite reservoirs. I then had to summon all of my strength as, unbeknown to her, I wasn't taking her back to her old house. We finished our lunch and got into my car as I turned up her all-time favourite song *Dancing Queen*. I took a deep breath and held back my tears as we began the next part of our journey. We were still singing our hearts out as we pulled into the car park of where she would be living from that moment on, a permanent care home.

Considering I have found approximately 75,000 words to write three books it surprises me that I cannot find the words to describe the emotional pain I have experienced whilst writing *Share Your World*. There are no words to describe losing my mum to such a cruel condition.

Dedicating *Share Your World* to my mum, knowing not only that she will never read my book but that tragically she no longer knows who I am is simply heart-breaking.

I have learnt my lesson the hard way.

I have shared this story with you in the hope that you will not make the same mistake.

My mum is only 71 years old. Nobody has the guarantee of tomorrow.

When I say that you can find a way, or you can find an excuse I truly mean it. With everything that has happened since I began writing *Share Your World* I could have found every excuse under the sun to put my pen down. This was never an option as I embody and live by all of the principles I have taught you.

Despite experiencing the hardest few months of my life, I feel incredibly fulfilled and content. I have not only found the strength and courage to write another book, I am mentoring authors whilst supporting my family and bringing up my incredible children Kieron and Lennie.

I am often asked where do I find the strength and determination to keep going? My mission is to create a new generation of heart-led authors who will all make a difference in the world, one book at a time. This is not just my business, this is my life purpose and I would be doing the world a disservice by not sharing my message. I have made a commitment to myself and I have made a commitment to you that *Share Your World* will be written and published as quickly as possible, no matter what.

I ask that you make the same commitment.

I want you to know that your book is going to make a difference in the world.

It will change many lives, starting with your own.

Life is not a fairy-tale, but you now have everything you need to *Share Your World* and create your very own happy ever after.

Cassandra x

Resources

To download your free author mediation please visit
www.cassandrafarren.com/free-meditations

Contact Cassandra

To find out more about Cassandra and her author mentoring programmes please visit:

www.cassandrafarren.com

You can connect with Cassandra on social media

Facebook/groups/heartledauthors

Facebook/cassandrafarren1

Linkedin/cassandrafarren.com

For speaking or press enquiries please e-mail

hello@cassandrafarren.com

Cassandra would love you to leave a review for *Share Your World* on Amazon.

Cassandra's First Book

The Girl Who Refused to Quit

The Girl Who Refused to Quit tells the surprisingly uplifting journey of a young woman who has overcome more than her fair share of challenges.

When she hit rock bottom for the third time Cassandra was left questioning her worth and her purpose. She could have been forgiven for giving up on everything. Instead she chose to transform adversity into triumph and with not much more than sheer determination Cassandra has now set up her own business to empower other women.

She is the girl who refused to be defined by her circumstances. She is the girl who wants to inspire other women, to show them that no matter what challenges you face you can still hold your head high, believe in yourself and follow your dreams.

She is The Girl Who Refused to Quit.

Available on Paperback & Kindle from Amazon.

Cassandra's Second Book

Rule Your World

Reduce Your Stress, Regain Your Control & Restore Your Calm

Have you ever questioned why your head is in such a mess – even when your life appears to look so good?

You know something needs to change, but don't know where to start?

When she became a single parent for the third time Cassandra feared her head may become a bigger mess than her life and inadvertently began to follow "The Rules".

Sharing her thought provoking and refreshing personal insights Cassandra's 7 rules will help to raise your self-awareness and empower a calmer, more fulfilling way of living.

Combining relatable real-life stories, and intriguing scientific studies with simple but powerful exercises, you will gain your own "Toolbox for Life" as well as admiration for this determined and strong woman.

Cassandra is living proof that when you reduce your stress, regain your control & restore your calm, you too can Rule Your World.

Available on Paperback & Kindle from Amazon.

9 780993 129667